P9-DSZ-764

A Pebble for Your Pocket

Mindful Stories for Children and Grown-ups

A Pebble
for Your Pocket

Mindful Stories for Children and Grown-ups

Thich Nhat Hanh

Plum Blossom Books
Berkeley, California

Plum Blossom Books
P.O. Box 7355
Berkeley, California 94707

Plum Blossom Books is an imprint of Parallax Press,
the publishing division of Unified Buddhist Church, Inc.

Original edition © 2001 by Unified Buddhist Church.
© 2010 by Unified Buddhist Church.
All Rights Reserved.
Printed in the United States of America.

Cover illustration by Philippe Ames.
Illustrations by Nguyen Thi Hop and Nguyen Dong (pp. 11, 14, 20, 39).
All other illustrations by Philippe Ames.
Cover and text design by Gopa & Ted2 Inc.
Back cover photograph by Simon Chaput.

Library of Congress Cataloging-in-Publication Data

Nhât Hanh, Thích.
  A pebble for your pocket : mindful stories for children and
grown-ups / Thich Nhat Hanh. — [Rev. ed.]
    p. cm.
  ISBN 978-1-935209-45-4
  1. Religious life--Buddhism--Juvenile literature. I. Title.
  BQ5405.N48 2010
  294.3'444083--dc22

                                          2010001769

1 2 3 4 5 / 14 13 12 11 10

Contents

Precious gems are everywhere in the cosmos
and inside of every one of us.
I want to offer a handful to you, my dear friend.
Yes, this morning, I want to offer a handful to you,
a handful of diamonds that glow from morning
   to evening.
Each minute of our daily life is a diamond that
   contains
sky and earth, sunshine and river.

—Thich Nhat Hanh

Introduction

When I was nine, I saw an image of the Buddha sitting peacefully on the grass on the cover of a magazine. Right away I knew that I wanted to be peaceful and happy like that too. Two years later, five of us boys were sitting together talking about what we wanted to be when we grew up. We explored many different fields; one boy said he wanted to be a doctor, another said an engineer, and so on. But after a while, we found that nothing really appealed to us.

Then my brother Nho said, "I want to become a monk." This was a novel idea, but I knew I also wanted to become a monk. In part it was because of the picture on the magazine.

Then one boy said, "Why don't we all become monks?" It was children's talk, but in fact all five of us did become monks. One boy became a Catholic monk, and the other four of us became Buddhist monks. And to this day, three of us are still monks.

The seed of becoming a monk was planted deeply in me after that discussion. I really wanted to become a monk, but I knew for my parents it would be difficult to accept because the life of a monk is a very modest one, and they wanted their children to enjoy the good things in life. I knew that I had to carefully prepare them.

I kept a diary, and from time to time I wrote about my aspiration to become a monk. One day I asked my mother to read my diary to my father so that they would get accustomed to the idea. It was too hard for me to do it directly. In that way, going slowly, step by step, I won the approval of my parents and was allowed to go to the temple. I became a novice at the age of sixteen.

Being a monk means that I spend a lot of time paying attention to the present moment. And everyone can live this way, whether or not you are a monk or nun. We call this "mindfulness." The stories in this book are all about mindfulness. There can be no happiness or peace without mindfulness. Mindfulness is remembering to come back to the present moment. Everything we are looking for is right here in the present moment. When we allow ourselves to be in the present moment, we have the capacity to touch all the wonderful things inside us and around us. But if we do not allow ourselves to be in the present moment, we will continue to run and to struggle.

Mindfulness helps us to live more happily and to see the beauty of things more deeply. When you look at the full moon with mindfulness, it is much more beautiful. When you hug someone with mindfulness, that person will be more real and sweet. You can say silently,

Breathing in, she's alive and in my arms.
Breathing out, I'm so happy.

Without mindfulness, you are not really alive. Being mindful makes everything you do seem brighter, more beautiful. When you look at a flower with mindfulness, the flower reveals its beauty to you. To practice mindfulness is to be happy and to enjoy what the moment brings you, including all the wonderful things inside of you—your eyes, your heart, your lungs—and all the wonderful things outside—sunshine, people, birds, trees. Practicing mindfulness, you will find that you have even more reasons to be happy than you thought.

Mindfulness also helps to heal pain. When pain comes in touch with mindfulness, the pain begins to slowly dissolve. If you have pain but don't know it, that pain will stay with you for a long time. But when you are aware of your pain and you embrace it with the arms of your mindfulness, then that pain begins to transform.

When you are in pain, you can use your mindfulness to hold your pain tenderly, just as a mother takes her crying baby into her arms to quiet him or her. If you embrace your pain in this way, it will transform. A crying baby should not be left unattended, and neither should your pain.

In the early morning, the flowers are closed, but when the sun shines, tiny particles of sunshine penetrate into the flowers, and you soon see a transformation. Each flower opens and shows itself to the sun. Our suffering is like that; if we expose it to the light of mindfulness, it will change.

Stories

✳

Who Is the Buddha?

Some years ago, I visited a village in India called Uruvela. Two thousand six hundred years ago, a man named Siddhartha lived near that village. Siddhartha is the man who later became known as the Buddha.

The village of Uruvela remains very much the same as it was back then. There are no big buildings, no supermarkets, no freeways. It is very pleasant. The children have not changed either. When Siddhartha lived there, children from that village became his friends and brought him food and simple gifts.

There is a river that runs near the village. It is where Siddhartha used to bathe. A grass called kusha grass still grows on the banks of the river. It is the same kind of grass that one of the children gave Siddhartha to use as a cushion to sit on. I walked across the river, and I cut some of the kusha grass and brought it home with me.

On the other side of the river, there is a forest. That is where Siddhartha sat in meditation under a tree called the Bodhi tree. It is under that tree that he became the Buddha.

A Buddha is anyone who is awake—who is aware of

everything that happens inside and around her—and who understands and loves deeply. Siddhartha became a fully awakened being, a Buddha. He is the Buddha that we have accepted as our teacher. He has said that each one of us has a seed of awakening within us and that all of us are future Buddhas.

When he was very young, a student of mine struggled with the question of "Who is the Buddha?" The student's name was Hu, and this is his story.

When Hu was six or seven years old, he asked his father and mother if he could become a monk. Hu loved going to the Buddhist temple. He used to go there with his parents on new moon and full moon days to offer flowers, bananas, mangoes, and all kinds of exotic fruit to the Buddha.

In the temple, Hu was always treated with kindness. When people came to the temple, they seemed more relaxed and friendly. Hu was also aware that the head monk liked him. He would give Hu a banana or a mango every time he came. So that's why Hu loved going to the temple.

One day he said, "Mommy, I want to become a monk and live in the temple." I think he wanted to become a monk because he liked to eat bananas. I don't blame him. In Vietnam, there are several kinds of bananas that are so delicious.

Even though he was young, his father and mother

decided to let him go to the temple as a novice. The head monk gave Hu a tiny brown robe to wear. In his nice new robe, he must have looked like a baby monk.

When he first became a monk, Hu believed that the Buddha loved bananas, mangoes, and tangerines because every time people came to the temple, they brought bananas, mangoes, tangerines, and other fruit, and placed them in front of the Buddha. In Hu's little head that could only mean that the Buddha loved fruit very much.

One evening, he waited in the temple until all the visitors had gone home. He stood very quietly outside the entrance of the Buddha Hall. He checked to make sure no one else was around. Then he peered into the Buddha Hall. The Buddha statue was as big as a real person. In Hu's very young mind, the statue was the Buddha.

Hu imagined that the Buddha sat very still all day long, and when the hall was empty, he reached out for a banana. Hu waited and watched, hoping to see the Buddha take one of the bananas piled in front of him. He waited for a long time, but he did not see the Buddha pick up a banana. He was baffled. He could not understand why the Buddha did not eat any of the bananas that people brought to him.

Hu did not dare ask the head monk, because he was afraid that the monk would think he was silly. Actually, we often feel like that. We do not dare ask questions because we are afraid we might be called silly. The same was true for Hu. And because he didn't dare ask, he was confused.

I think I would have gone to someone and asked. But Hu did not ask anyone.

As he grew older, one day it occurred to him that the Buddha statue was not the Buddha. What an achievement!

This realization made him so happy. But then a new question arose. "If the Buddha is not here, then where is he? If the Buddha is not in the temple, where is the Buddha?" Every day he saw people come to the temple and bow to the statue of the Buddha. But where was the Buddha?

In Vietnam, people who practice Pure Land Buddhism believe that the Buddhas stay in the Pure Land, in the direction of the West. One day, Hu overheard someone saying that the Pure Land was the home of the Buddhas. This made Hu believe that the Buddha was in the Pure Land, which made him very unhappy. Why, he wondered, did the Buddha choose to live so far away from people? So this created another question in his mind.

I met Hu when he was fourteen, and he was still wondering about this. I explained to him that the Buddha is not far away from us. I told him that the Buddha is inside each one of us. Being a Buddha is being aware of what is inside of us and around us at every moment. Buddha is the love and understanding that we each carry in our hearts. This made Hu very happy.

When Hu grew up, he became the director of the School of Social Work in Vietnam. He trained young nuns and monks, young men and women, to help people rebuild the villages that had been bombed during the Vietnam War.

Anywhere you see love and understanding, there is the Buddha. Anyone can be a Buddha. Do not imagine that the Buddha is a statue or someone who has a fancy halo around his or her head or wears a yellow robe. A Buddha is a person who is aware of what is going on inside and around him or her and has a lot of understanding and compassion. Whether a Buddha is a man or a woman, young or not so young, a Buddha is always very pleasant and fresh.

The Many Arms of a Bodhisattva

In my experience, there are Buddhas and bodhisattvas present here, in our midst. A bodhisattva (pronounced "bo-dee-*sat*-va") is a compassionate person, someone who cares a lot about helping other beings—someone who vows to become a Buddha.

Statues or pictures of bodhisattvas sometimes show a being with many arms. They are shown this way because a bodhisattva is someone who can do a thousand things at one time. Also, the arms of a bodhisattva can be extremely long and reach very far, helping people in faraway lands. With only two arms, we can only do one or two things at a time. But when you are a bodhisattva, you have many arms, and you can do many things simultaneously. Most of the time, we do not see all the arms of a bodhisattva. One has to be very attentive in order to see the many arms of a bodhisattva.

You may already know someone who is a bodhisattva. It is possible! Your mom, for example, could be a bodhisattva. She does many things at the same time. She needs

an arm for cooking. Isn't that true? But at the same time she takes care of you and your brothers and sisters—so she needs a second arm. And then at the same time, she has to run errands. So she needs a third arm. And she has many other things she does that require more arms—she may have a job or she may volunteer at your school. So your mom could be a bodhisattva. The same is true for your dad. Look more deeply at your mother and father and you will see that they have more than two arms.

Do not think that Buddhas and bodhisattvas are beings who exist in heaven. They are right here, all around us. You too can be a bodhisattva if you think of others and do things to bring happiness to them.

If you are awake, if you are present in the moment, here and now, you too are a Buddha. The only difference between you and the Buddha is that he is a full-time Buddha. You are only a part-time Buddha. So you have to live in a way that gives the baby Buddha inside you a chance to grow. Then the baby Buddha will radiate light in all the cells of your body, and you will begin to give off this light.

The Hermit and the Well

I would like to tell you the story of my encounter with the Buddha inside me. When I was a child like you, I lived in North Vietnam, in the province of Thanh Hoa. When I was nine years old, I found a magazine with a black and white drawing of the Buddha on the cover. He was sitting on the grass. He sat beautifully. He looked very peaceful and happy. His face was calm and relaxed, with a little smile. I looked at that picture of the Buddha, and it made me feel very peaceful too.

As a little boy, I noticed that the people around me were not usually that calm and peaceful. So when I saw the Buddha, looking so peaceful and happy just sitting on the grass, I wanted to be like him. Even though I did not know anything about the Buddha or his life, when I saw that picture, I felt love for him. After that, I had a strong desire to become someone who could sit as he did, beautifully and peacefully.

One day when I was eleven, my teacher at school announced that we were going to the top of Na Son Mountain to have a picnic. I had never been there before. The teacher told us that at the top of the mountain there lived a hermit. He explained that a hermit was someone who lived alone and practiced day and night to become like the Buddha. How fascinating! I had never seen a hermit before, and I became very excited at the prospect of climbing the mountain and meeting him.

The day before the outing, we prepared food for the picnic. We cooked rice, rolled it into balls, and wrapped the balls in banana leaves. We prepared sesame seeds, peanuts, and salt to dip the rice in. You may never have eaten a rice ball dipped in sesame seeds, peanuts, and salt, but I can tell you it is very delicious. We also boiled water to drink, because it was not safe to drink water straight from the river. Having fresh water to drink is wonderful too.

One hundred and fifty students from my school went on the field trip together. We split up into groups of five. Carrying our picnic with us, we walked for a long time, nearly ten miles, before we reached the foot of the mountain. Then we began our climb.

There were many beautiful trees and rocks along the path. But we did not enjoy them much because we were so anxious to reach the top of the mountain. My friends and I climbed as quickly as we could—we practically ran all the way up the mountain. When I was little, I did not know, as I do now, about the joy of walking meditation—not hurrying, just enjoying each step, the flowers, the trees, the blue sky, and the company of friends.

When my friends and I reached the top, we were

exhausted. We had drunk all of our water on the way up and did not have even a drop left. Still, I was very eager to find the hermit. We found his hut made of bamboo and straw. Inside, we saw a small bamboo cot and a bamboo altar, but no one was there. What a disappointment! I thought that the hermit must have heard that many boys were coming up the mountain, and since he did not like a lot of talking and noise, he had hidden somewhere.

It was time to have lunch, but I didn't care to eat because I was so tired and disappointed. I thought that maybe if I wandered into the forest I would have a chance to find the hermit. When I was little I had a lot of hope—anything was possible.

So I left my friends and started climbing further up the mountain. As I walked through the forest, I heard the sound of dripping water. You have probably heard it too. It is like the sound of wind chimes or a piano being softly played—very clear and light, like crystal. It was so appealing and peaceful that I started to climb in the direction of the lovely sound, driven also by my great thirst.

It was not long before I came upon a natural well made of stones. I knew that spring water comes up from deep inside the earth. Where the water came up, a natural well made of big rocks of many colors surrounded the spring to form a small pool. The water was high, and so clear that I could see all the way to the bottom. The water looked so fresh and inviting that I knelt down, scooped some in my palms, and began to drink. You cannot imagine my happiness. The water tasted wonderfully sweet. It was so delicious, so refreshing! I felt completely satisfied. I did not have any desire left in me—even the desire to meet the hermit was gone. It is the most wonderful feeling, the feeling of bliss, when you don't desire anything anymore.

Suddenly, it occurred to me that maybe I had met the hermit after all. I began to think that the hermit had magical powers, that he had transformed himself into the well so that I could meet him, and that he cared about me. This made me happy.

I lay down on the ground next to the well and looked up at the sky. I saw the branch of a tree against the blue sky. I was so relaxed, and soon I fell into a deep sleep. I don't know how long I slept, maybe only three or four minutes. When I awoke, I didn't know where I was. When I saw the branch of the tree against the sky and the wonderful well, I remembered everything.

It was time to go back to join the other boys or they might begin to worry about me. I said good-bye to the well and began to walk back down. As I walked out of the forest, a sentence formed in my heart. It was like a poem with only one line: "I have tasted the most delicious water in the world!" I will always remember these words.

My friends were glad to see me when I returned. They were laughing and talking loudly, but I had no desire to talk. I was not yet ready to share my experience of the hermit

and the well with the other boys. What had happened was something very precious and sacred, and I wanted to keep it to myself. I sat down on the ground and ate my lunch quietly. The rice and the sesame seeds tasted so good. I felt calm and happy and peaceful.

I met my hermit in the form of a well. The image of the well and the sound of dripping water are still alive in me today. You too may have met your hermit, perhaps not as a well but as something else equally marvelous. Perhaps it was a rock, a tree, a star, or a beautiful sunset. The hermit is the Buddha inside of you.

Maybe you haven't met your hermit yet, but if you look deeply, your hermit will be revealed to you. I have invited children to write to me when they meet their hermit and some of them have. It always makes me so happy to read the stories of their encounters with their hermit. The hermit is inside of you. In fact, all the wonderful things that you are looking for—happiness, peace, and joy—can be found inside of you. You do not need to look anywhere else.

Present Moment, Wonderful Moment

"Life is available only in the present moment." This is a simple teaching of the Buddha, but very deep. If someone asked you, "Has the best moment of your life arrived yet?" many of you would probably say that the best moment of your life has not yet come. We all have a tendency to believe that the best moment of our lives has not yet come, but that it will come very soon. But if we continue to live in the same way, waiting for the best moment to arrive, then the best moment will never arrive.

You may believe that your happiness is somewhere else, over there, or in the future, but in fact you can touch your happiness right now. You are alive. You can open your eyes, you can see the sunshine, the beautiful color of the sky, the wonderful vegetation, your friends and relatives around you. This is the best moment of your life!

Today's Day

We have all sorts of special days. There is a special day to remember fathers. We call it Father's Day. There is a special day to celebrate our mothers. We call it Mother's Day. There is New Year's Day, Peace Day, and Earth Day. One day a young person visiting Plum Village said, "Why not declare today as 'Today's Day'?" And all the children agreed that we should celebrate today and call it "Today's Day."

On this day, Today's Day, we don't think about yesterday, we don't think about tomorrow, we only think about today. Today's Day is when we live happily in the present moment. When we eat, we know that we are eating. When we drink water, we are aware that it is water we are drinking. When we walk, we really enjoy each step. When we play, we are really present in our play.

Today is a wonderful day. Today is the most wonderful day. That does not mean that yesterday was not wonderful. But yesterday is already gone. It does not mean that tomorrow will not be wonderful. But tomorrow is not yet here. Today is the only day available to us today, and we can take good care of it. That is why today is so important— the most important day of our lives.

So each morning when you wake up, decide to make that day the most important day. Before you go off to school, sit or lie down, breathe slowly in and out for a few minutes, enjoy your in-breath, enjoy your out-breath, and smile. You are here. You are content. You are peaceful. This is a wonderful way to begin a day.

Try to keep this spirit alive all day. Remember to go back to your breath and be aware of your in- and out-breath,

remember to look at other people with loving kindness, remember to smile and to be happy for the gift of life. Then when you say, "Have a good day today," this is not only a wish, it is a reality, it is a practice.

Enjoying Our Food

Many times when we are eating our food, we are thinking of other things and we don't really know what it is we are eating. When we know what we are eating, it can be so enjoyable. To be able to eat gives us great happiness. To have something to eat every day is a great happiness. Many people in the world do not have anything to eat. We do our best to put on our plate only what we can eat so that we do not waste food. When we chew our food slowly, we digest it better and enjoy it more. When we eat mindfully and enjoy each bite we are also more in touch with our bodies and know when we are really satisfied. Then we avoid overeating or eating food that is not good for us.

You might consider saying, "Dad, I'm so happy. The casserole tonight is wonderful. Thank you." This kind of talking will bring about more happiness. If you blame someone at the table, if you criticize someone, saying, "Why did you come home so late tonight?" it causes unhappiness for everyone. We have to live in such a way that sitting down to eat with our family becomes the happiest time of the day.

If you can create happiness when you eat, you can create happiness in other moments of the day, and that's a wonderful thing to know about yourself. You have the gift of creating happiness at any moment.

When you sit down to eat, look at your food and know

what it is that you are picking up to put into your mouth. If it is a carrot, see that it is a carrot that you are chewing and nothing else. If it is spaghetti, see that it is spaghetti and nothing else—not your anger, not your thoughts about what you are going to do tomorrow.

It only takes half a second to look at a carrot or spaghetti and recognize what you are about to eat. "This is a carrot." "This is spaghetti." It's very important to do this. When you look at the food you are eating and it still does not reveal itself to you, call it by its name: "Carrot," or "Spaghetti." After you call its name, the food will suddenly reveal itself to you.

If you continue to do this, over time you will begin to see the food that you are eating very deeply. Then one day you will see the sunshine, the rain cloud, and all the things and people that have come together to make the spaghetti and carrot in front of you.

When you put food in your mouth and chew it with this kind of awareness, you are chewing something wonderful. When you are truly present with your food, when you eat with all your heart and body, you connect with the whole cosmos. You have the sunshine, the clouds, the earth, time, and space in your mouth. You are in touch with reality, with life.

After eating plums, a child at Plum Village had this to say:

One day after we ate plums, we examined the pits. I noticed things that I had never seen before, like the various cracks that each pit had. I also noticed that most of them had ridges. In the past, I just threw away the pits. A few of us were able to split them open, and in the middle there is a very small seed. It's really neat. I had never split open a plum pit before. It helped me to be in the moment. I didn't just throw my pit away and go off looking for something else to do. We also realized that inside each pit there were thousands of plum trees.

Return to Your Hermitage

O ne day I decided to go to the beautiful woods near my hermitage, the place where I live. I took a sandwich and a blanket with me, intending to spend a quiet day by myself.

That morning, before leaving the hermitage, I had opened all my windows and doors to the sun to dry things out. But in the afternoon the weather changed. The wind began to blow and dark clouds gathered in the sky. Remembering that I had left my hermitage wide open, I decided to return home right away.

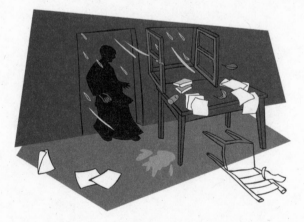

When I arrived, I found my hermitage in a very terrible condition. It was cold and dark inside. The wind had blown my papers off the table, and they were scattered all over the floor. It was not at all pleasant. ·

The first thing I did was to close all the windows and doors. Then I lit the lamp for some light. The third thing I did was to make a fire in the fireplace to warm the place up. When the fire was lit, I picked up the papers from the floor and put them on the table and placed a stone on them.

Then I went back to the fireplace. The fire was burning beautifully. Now there was light, and I was warm. I sat there and listened to the wind howling outside. I imagined the trees tossing in the wind, and I felt very content. It was pleasant sitting next to the fire. I could hear my breathing, my in-breath and my out-breath. I felt very comfortable.

There are moments in our daily lives when we feel miserable, very empty and cold, and we are not happy. It seems that everything is going wrong. You too have prob-ably experienced a feeling like this at some point in your life. Even when we try to make the situation better with things we do or say, nothing seems to work, and we think, "This is not my day." That is exactly how my hermitage was that day.

The best thing to do at a time like this is to go back to yourself, to your hermitage, close all the windows and doors, light a lamp, and make a fire. This means that you have come to a stop. You are no longer busy looking at things, hearing things, or saying things. You have gone back to yourself and become one with your breathing. That is what going back to your hermitage means.

Each of you has a hermitage to go to inside—a place to take refuge and breathe. But this does not mean that you are cutting yourself off from the world. It means that you are getting more in touch with yourself. Breathing is a good way of doing this. Try it. Just stop where you are and notice your in-breath and your out-breath. With the in-breath, say to yourself, "Breathing in, I am in the present moment." And with the out-breath, say to yourself, "Breathing out, it is a wonderful moment." As you repeat these lines, you can simply use the words "present moment" for the in-breath, and "wonderful moment" for the out-breath. Breathing this way can make you feel really wonderful inside.

Stopping and breathing like this is called mindful breathing or breathing meditation. Breathing mindfully will make your hermitage a lot more comfortable. And when your hermitage inside is comfortable, then your contact with the world outside of you will become more pleasant.

When We Are Angry

When something unpleasant happens, you may become very angry or upset. Maybe your sister or brother does or says something you don't like. When you are very angry, usually you just want to scream at the other person or cry.

Because we feel hurt, we want to say or do something to hurt that person back. We think that by saying something cruel back to him or her, we will feel better. But when we say hurtful words back, that person will look for something even more cruel to say. And neither person knows how to stop.

When someone makes you angry, it is better not to respond with words. The first thing to do is to stop and return to your breathing. That's what I do. I say, "Breathing in, I know I am angry. Breathing out, anger is still there." I continue to breathe like this for three or four breaths, and then usually there is a slight change in me, a softening of the anger inside.

We can learn how to act in a way that does not create

unhappiness for ourselves or those around us. We can learn to change an unhappy situation into a joyful one. It requires some practice, however. Even though we learn a lot at school, we do not have the opportunity to learn how to be happy or how to suffer less.

Our anger is a part of us. We should not pretend that we are not angry when in fact we are angry. What we need to learn is how to take care of our anger. A good way to take care of our anger is to stop and return to our breathing.

Think of your anger as your little baby brother or sister. No matter what your baby brother or baby sister has done, you have to treat him or her with tenderness and love. In the same way, you need to treat your anger with tenderness and love. When you are angry, say:

Breathing in, I know that I am angry.
Breathing out, I am taking good care of
    my anger.

While you are breathing and saying this, you may still be angry. But you are safe, because you are embracing your anger the way a mother embraces her crying baby. After doing this for a while, your temper will begin to calm down and you will be able to smile at your anger:

Breathing in, I see anger in me.
Breathing out, I smile at my anger.

When we take care of our anger like this, we are being mindful. Mindfulness acts just like the rays of the sun. Without any effort, the sun shines on everything and everything changes because of it. When we expose our anger to the light of mindfulness, it will change too, like a flower opening to the sun.

A Pebble for Your Pocket

Sometimes when we become angry during the day, it is difficult to remember to stop and breathe. I know a good way for you to remember to stop and breathe when you are angry or upset. First, go for a walk and find a pebble that you like. Then, go sit near the Buddha if there is one in your house, or outside under a special tree or on a special rock, or go to your room. With the pebble in your hand, say:

Dear Buddha,
Here is my pebble. I am going to practice with it when things go wrong in my day. Whenever I am angry or upset, I will take the pebble in my hand and breathe deeply. I will do this until I calm down.

Now put your pebble in your pocket and take it with you wherever you go. When something happens during the day that makes you unhappy, put your hand in your pocket, take hold of the pebble, breathe deeply, and say to yourself, "Breathing in, I know I am angry. Breathing out, I am taking good care of my anger." Do this until you feel a lot better and can smile to your anger.

Walking Mindfully

Another wonderful way to calm down when we are upset is by walking. As we walk, we pay attention to each step we take. We notice how each foot touches the ground. The Earth is our mother. When we are away from Mother Nature, we get sick. Each step we take allows us to touch our mother, so that we can be well again. A lot of harm has been done to Mother Earth, so now it is time to kiss the Earth with our feet, with our love.

During your walk, stop to observe the beautiful things around you, above you, and below you. Continue to breathe in and out in order to get in touch with these wonderful things. The moment you stop being aware of your breathing, the beautiful things may vanish, and thinking and worrying may settle in your mind again.

Just allow yourself to be! Allow yourself to enjoy being in the present moment. The Earth is so beautiful. Enjoy the

planet Earth. You are beautiful too, you are a marvel like the Earth. To walk like this is called walking meditation.

Remember that while you are walking, you are not going anywhere, yet every step helps you to arrive. To arrive where? To arrive in the present moment, to arrive in the here and now. You don't need anything else to be happy. Some of the children at Plum Village expressed it this way:

✳ Walking meditation is so you notice everything around you. You listen to your breath. If you don't ever walk mindfully, your whole life can pass by without you noticing it. Think what a pity it would be if you passed through your life thinking only about what is going to happen next and never noticed anything else, never knew what the world was like at all. That would be pretty sad.

✳ It involves a lot of patience to be mindful. When you are mindful, your mind is full of the things around you, full of your breathing, feeling the rocks under your feet, and that's mindfulness. You are in the present moment, you are aware of what you are doing. You know that you are walking, and that you are walking with Thay. Your mind can't be somewhere else, thinking about eating dinner. It has to be right where you are. And that's walking meditation.

✳ I think that what is special about walking medita-tion is that you can notice everything around you. You take everything in, like the blue sky. We can be in touch with many, many wonderful things.

The Lotus Pond

I n Plum Village, where I live in France, there is a beautiful lotus pond. Maybe one day you will come to Plum Village and you can see it. In the summer the pond is covered with hundreds of beautiful lotus blossoms. What is amazing is that all the lotus plants in the pond come from a single tiny seed. I will tell you how to grow a lotus pond.

Lotus seeds have to be planted in wet soil. They do not grow well in dry soil. But there is a trick to planting a lotus seed. If you just put the seed into the mud, it will not sprout, even if you wait three weeks, five weeks, or ten weeks. But it will not die, either. There are lotus seeds more than one thousand years old that when planted properly have grown into lotus plants.

The lotus seed does not sprout if you just place it in the mud because the lotus seed needs some help to sprout. The lotus seed is a kernel with very hard skin covering it. In order to sprout, water needs to penetrate into the lotus seed through the hard skin. That is the trick. You need to make a little hole in the seed so that the water can get in.

You can pierce the outer skin by cutting into it with a knife or by rubbing it against a rock. This will give water

a chance to penetrate into the seed. Now if you place it in the water or in the mud, in about four or five days the tiny seed will sprout and become a tiny lotus plant.

At first a few small lotus leaves will appear. Soon they will grow bigger. You can keep a little lotus plant in your yard during the spring, summer, or autumn. But when it is cold, you have to bring it inside, where it will continue to grow.

In the spring you can bring it out again and put it in a larger container, and the lotus plant will grow even bigger. In one year you will have a few lotus flowers, and in three years you will have a lotus pond as big as the one in Plum Village.

So you see, a huge lotus pond truly is contained within one tiny seed. This tiny seed contains all the ancestors of the lotus plant—it contains their fragrance and beauty, all their characteristics. As this seed sprouts and begins to grow, it offers all these gifts to the world.

Each of you is a wonderful seed like the lotus seed. You look a little bigger than a lotus seed, but you are a seed nonetheless. In you there is understanding and love and many, many different talents. From our ancestors we receive wonderful seeds. Our ability to play music or paint, to run fast or do math, to make things with our hands or dance are all seeds we receive from our ancestors. We also inherit seeds that are not so nice, like the seeds of fear and anger. These seeds of fear and anger can make us very unhappy, and often we don't know what to do.

Some time ago, a twelve-year-old Swiss boy and his sister started coming regularly to Plum Village. The boy had a problem with his father: he was very angry with his father because his father did not speak kindly to him. Whenever the boy fell down or hurt himself, instead of helping and comforting him, his father got angry with him. He would say, "You're stupid! Why did you do such a thing?"

The boy, of course, wanted his father to comfort him with kind words when he was in pain. He could not understand why his father treated him this way, and he vowed that he would never act like his father when he grew up. If he had a son, he would help him up and comfort him should he fall and hurt himself.

One day, this boy was watching his sister play on a hammock with another girl. They were swinging back and forth. Suddenly, the hammock turned over and both girls fell to the ground. His sister cut her forehead. When the boy saw his sister bleeding, he became furious. He was about to shout at her, "You're stupid! Why did you hurt yourself like that?" But because he knew how to practice, he caught himself, and went back to his breathing. Seeing that his sister was all right and was being taken care of by others, he decided to do walking meditation.

During his walking meditation, he discovered something

wonderful. He saw that he was exactly like his father. He had the same kind of energy that pushed him to say unkind words. When your loved ones are suffering, you should be loving, tender, and helpful, and not shout at them out of anger. He saw that he was about to behave exactly like his father. That was his insight. Imagine a twelve-year-old boy practicing like that. He realized he was the continuation of his father and had the same kind of energy, the same negative seeds.

Continuing to walk mindfully, he discovered that he could not transform his anger without practice, and that if he did not practice, he would transmit the same energy of anger to his children. I think it is remarkable for a twelve-year-old boy to succeed like this in meditation. He gained these two insights in less than fifteen minutes of walking meditation.

His third and final insight was that when he returned home he would discuss his discoveries with his father. He decided to ask his father to practice with him so that both of them could transform their energy. With this third insight, his anger at his father vanished because he understood that his father was also a victim. His father might have received this energy from his own father. So you see, the practice of looking deeply to gain understanding and freedom from your anger is very important.

The Precious Gem

I n Buddhism, there is an image of the world that is very wonderful. The image shows a world full of bright, shiny jewels. This world is called the Dharmakaya (pronounced "Dar-ma-*ka*-ya"). The Dharmakaya is not separate from the world we see everyday. When we look closely, we will discover that our everyday world is full of wonderful treasures. Long ago, Buddha told a story to remind us that these wonderful treasures are always there for us, if only we are able to see them.

Once there was a rich man who had a very lazy son. The young man didn't know how to do anything except spend his father's money. Because he was the son of a rich man, he had never learned a trade and did not know how to make a living.

The father was afraid that after he died, his son would sell everything in the house and become a pauper. Although he tried very hard to change his son, in the end the father realized that this would not happen in his lifetime.

Yet the father loved his son very much, and he could not stop worrying about him. Then, one evening after much thought, he had an idea. The next morning, he went to his tailor and asked him to make a warm jacket. When the jacket was finished, the old man took it home and wore it everyday until it began to look used.

One day, he called his son to him and said, "My son, when I die you will inherit everything that I have. I hope that you will manage your inheritance well. If, however, you decide to sell my belongings, I ask just one thing." Picking up his jacket, he said, "I ask that you keep this jacket and wear it all the time. This will be enough to make me happy."

The son looked at his father's worn jacket. This he could easily do.

"Don't worry, Father, I promise I will not sell it."

Soon after that the father died, and the young man inherited all his father's wealth. And just as his father had anticipated, the son sold all his belongings. He kept his promise, however, and did not sell the jacket.

It was not long before the son had spent all the money he had received from selling his father's valuables. And as his father had feared, his son became very poor. One by one, his friends abandoned him. And since he did not know how to make a living for himself, he soon became homeless.

Without a home or friends, the son began to wander from place to place. Many nights he had to sleep outside under a tree without dinner. But he still had his father's jacket to keep him warm.

Many years passed and the son still wandered from place to place without a roof over his head. Then one day, while he was lying on the ground, he felt something hard under his body. At first he thought it was a stone on the ground beneath him. But when he looked, there was no stone.

Determined to find out what the hard thing was, he checked inside the pockets of the jacket he was wearing, but there was nothing. He became more curious, and he searched the entire jacket. Suddenly he felt something inside the lining of the threadbare jacket. He cut into the lining and, to his surprise, out dropped a gem. His father had put a precious gem in the lining of the jacket!

After so many years of thinking that he was poor, the son realized that he was rich. But now he had learned his lesson. He would not squander his inheritance this time. He bought a house and started a business. He began to earn his living. He was overjoyed! Grateful that he had a second chance, he was happy to share his wealth with others.

After telling this story, the Buddha said that we are all like the son. We too have inherited great wealth, but like the son, we don't know it and we behave as if we were poor. We have a treasure of enlightenment, understanding, love, and joy inside us. And if we know how to rediscover them and allow them to manifest, we shall be extremely happy.

There are many chances for us to be happy. But we keep thinking that we are only a destitute son or daughter.

So it is time to go back to receive your inheritance. Being mindful will help you claim it. With mindfulness you will see that you have many gems in the lining of your jacket. You need only to look up in order to see the blue sky. You need only to breathe in and out to see that today is beautiful and worth living. You need only to breathe in and out to see that those you love are still alive around you, and you can be very, very happy.

This is a poem I wrote after I read the Buddha's story about the rich man and his son:

> Precious gems are everywhere in the cosmos
> and inside of every one of us.
>
> I want to offer a handful to you, my dear friend.
> Yes, this morning, I want to offer a handful
>   to you,
> a handful of diamonds that glow from morning to
>   evening.
> Each minute of our daily life is a diamond
> that contains sky and earth, sunshine and river.
>
> We only need to breathe gently for the miracle to be
>   revealed:
> birds singing, flowers blooming.

Here is the blue sky, here is the white cloud floating,
your lovely look, your beautiful smile.
All these are contained in one jewel.

You who are the richest person on Earth
And behave like a destitute son,
please come back to your heritage.

Let us offer each other happiness
and learn to dwell in the present moment.
Let us cherish life in our two arms
and let go of our forgetfulness and despair.

You Are a Buddha-to-Be

The name "Buddha" comes from the Sanskrit word "budh," which means to awaken, to understand, and to know. A Buddha is one who is awake, who is aware of everything that happens in the present moment. The depth of his or her understanding and love is very great. Anybody can become a Buddha. We are all future Buddhas, capable of having deep understanding and a great ability to love and relieve the suffering of others.

Friends of the Buddha often greet each other by joining their hands to make a lotus bud. The lotus is a beautiful flower that looks like a magnolia. We put our palms together while breathing in, and silently say, "A lotus for you." Then we bow, breathe out, and silently say, "A Buddha-to-be." When we make this gesture, we acknowledge the presence of the other person and offer them our own presence.

The Buddha said that there are many Buddhas everywhere who are teaching at this very moment, trying to bring love and compassion into everyday life. The Buddha said that all of us are Buddhas-to-be. He was right, because in each of us there are seeds of understanding, love, and compassion. When we cultivate love and understanding, we are watering those seeds, and they will blossom and bear fruit. If we practice according to the teachings of the Buddha, we too will become Buddhas.

Each of us is a Buddha-to-be. That is why we want to live in a way that allows the Buddha in us to blossom. When we know how to breathe, how to walk, how to smile, how to treat people, plants, animals, and minerals, we become real Buddhas.

Respecting Your Body and Mind

If you think of yourself as a Buddha-to-be, it will help you remember to take care of your body. Some parts of our bodies are very sacred. The top of the head is an altar for Asian people, especially the Vietnamese. We put the most sacred things on our altars. When we enter a house in Vietnam, even if it is very poor, there is always an ancestral altar with fruit, flowers, or incense. We treat an altar with great care; it is something sacred. Similarly, there are sacred parts of our bodies that we don't want anyone to see or touch. This is true for girls and boys. We can hold someone's hand or put our hand on someone's shoulder, but we should not touch the sacred areas of someone's body.

There are also sacred areas in the soul that we don't want anyone to see or touch. Especially as we get a little bit older, we find that there are experiences and images that we want to keep for ourselves. We don't want to share these with just anybody, only someone in whom we have the utmost confidence, the person we love the most. We reveal these confidences from the depths of our hearts to a very small number of people—maybe only one person. Only when we have a friend who really understands us can we share these things. This deep understanding comes from practicing to listen deeply and speak lovingly.

Be Kind to Yourself

Part of respecting our bodies is being mindful of what we take into our bodies and minds. Some of the things we eat and drink may make us feel good at first. But sometimes these feelings can lead to addiction and cause you much suffering. Please don't let seemingly pleasant feelings fool you. You have to look with mindfulness into these feelings, because they may contain the seeds of painful feelings that will manifest in you later on.

Consciousness is also a food. Believe it or not, when you read a magazine article, watch television, or go to the movies, you are ingesting consciousness, because these things reflect the collective consciousness of a group of people, with views, feelings, and so on. The Buddha said you have to be aware of the kind of consciousness you are ingesting. Some forms of consciousness are not good or healthy for you.

For example, a television program, a book, or even the news we read in the newspaper can bring toxins into our consciousness, and our fear, distress, and despair can be fed by such sights, sounds, and information. That is why you need to mindfully select and take in nourishment that will lead to your healing and transformation.

Mindful consumption means we bring into our body and mind only healthy food. We practice mindful eating, drinking, and consuming, and we avoid taking in toxins. We practice for ourselves and for the people in our family and society. The support of our family and friends can help us to do this.

Stopping

There is a well-known Zen story about a man on a galloping horse. Someone watching him ride by shouts to him, "Where are you going?" The rider turns and shouts, "I don't know, ask the horse."

This story is funny, but it is also true, because we don't know exactly where we are going or why we are rushing. A galloping horse is pushing us and deciding everything for us. And we follow. That horse is called "habit energy." You may have received this energy from your parents or your ancestors.

For example, even though we know that if we say something mean we'll create suffering for ourselves and for those around us, we still say it. Later we may regret it and say, "I couldn't help it; the urge was stronger than me." And we sincerely promise ourselves that the next time we will not say mean things. But when the situation arises again, we do exactly the same thing: we say and do things that are hurtful not only to others but to ourselves as well. This is what is meant by habit energy.

Our task then is to become aware of this habit energy

and not to let it push us around anymore. We can smile at it and say, "Hello there, my habit energy, I know you are there." So, the first way to take care of yourself is to learn how to stop and look inside. This is a very wonderful practice.

When we become agitated, when someone is angry or shouting, when we are very sad or depressed, what can we do to smile again and feel alive? If we learn the art of stopping, we can calm things down within and around us. The purpose of stopping is to become calm and solid and to see clearly. If we are not calm, solid, and clear-sighted, then we can't confront our problems.

Stopping doesn't mean sitting still. Even when you sit still in one place, your mind can be drawn into thinking about the past, the future, or about your projects; and that is not stopping. Inside of us there is a video that plays all the time, nonstop; we're always thinking of this or that, seeing one image after another. It never stops.

So even if you aren't saying anything aloud, there's still no silence within. Silence inside helps us enjoy what is here in the present moment. It allows us to look at the sunset and really enjoy it. It allows us to appreciate the presence of those we love.

So, stopping is going back to the here and now and touching the wonders of life that are always available. Without stopping, your mind is not unified with your body—your

body may be sitting in one place, but your mind is somewhere else. Stopping brings your body and mind together,
back to the here and now.

An important part of our practice is looking deeply in
order to see. We often suffer because we don't look carefully, and therefore we have misperceptions. It is like
someone walking on a path at night and suddenly seeing
a snake, and then running into the house screaming, "A
snake!" Everyone runs outside and when they shine a light
on the path, they see that the "snake" is really only a piece
of rope. So in order to take care of ourselves, and to calm
things down inside and around us, we practice stopping
and looking deeply.

By stopping the activities of your mind and body—just
sitting quietly, breathing in and out, being silent within—
you become more solid, more concentrated, and more
intelligent. Your mind is clear, and you react well because
you are solid and strong. Now you can look deeply at what
is happening inside and around you.

Under the Rose Apple Tree

Sitting meditation is one of the ways to return to the here
and now. If we know how to practice sitting meditation,
we will become clear, strong, and solid. Then it will not
be easy for anyone to provoke us or to make us lose our

composure. So you sit like a mountain. No wind can blow the mountain over. If you cannot sit for half an hour, sit for only three minutes. If you can sit like a mountain for three minutes, that is already very good.

When you sit, make sure that you are not sitting to please anyone else. Sit for yourself. When someone asks me, "Why do you sit?" I say, "Because I like it." If someone asks you why you sit, say, "I sit because I like it." I think that is the best answer. You enjoy sitting because you become a flower, a mountain, still water, and empty space. When you become all these wonderful things, you become truly yourself, living deeply in the here and now.

Here is a story about Siddhartha, the Buddha, when he was a boy.

When Siddhartha was nine years old, he and his schoolmates were allowed to attend the ceremony of the first plowing of the fields. Each year King Suddhodana, Siddhartha's father, presided over this ceremony. Gotami, Siddhartha's aunt and step-mother, dressed Siddhartha in his finest clothes for the occasion.

The ceremony was held in one of the most fertile fields in the kingdom. The priests began the ceremony by reciting from the holy scriptures. Then the king, with the help of two military officers, plowed the first row of the field as the crowd cheered them on. The plowing season had begun! Following the king's lead, the farmers began to plow their own fields.

Siddhartha stood at the edge of one of the fields and watched a farmer hitch a water buffalo to his plow. The farmer used one hand to steady the plow, and with the other hand he used a stick to urge on the water buffalo. The buffalo strained hard under the weight of the heavy plow. The sun blazed down on the farmer, his body glistening with sweat. The plow divided the rich earth into two neat furrows.

Siddhartha noticed that as the earth was turned by the plow, worms and other small creatures were being cut in half and left to die in the hot sun. Birds flying overhead spotted them and came to feast. A hawk swooped down, grasped one of the smaller birds in its talons, and carried it off.

Standing beneath the burning sun watching these events, Siddhartha, too, became drenched in sweat. He ran to the shade of a rose apple tree to reflect on the scene that had unfolded before him. He sat down and crossed his legs. He closed his eyes. He sat for a long time, still and straight, thinking about what he had seen in the field. As he sat there, family members began coming to the field with refreshments to celebrate the occasion of the first plowing. There was singing and dancing. But even after the festivities began, Siddhartha continued to sit quietly.

Siddhartha was still sitting, absorbed by what he had seen in the field, when the king and queen passed by. They were surprised to see Siddhartha sitting with such deep concentration. His stepmother was moved to tears when she saw how beautiful Siddhartha looked. When she approached him, the boy looked up and said, "Mother, reciting the scriptures does nothing to help the worms and the birds."

Later, when the Buddha had been practicing for a long time, he thought back to when he was nine years old and sat in meditation for the first time beneath the cool shade of the rose apple tree on the day of the year's first plowing, and he recalled how refreshing and peaceful those moments had been!

If sitting were unpleasant and required a lot of effort, I would not sit at all. I sit only because it makes me happy. I would not sit if it made me suffer. To sit in meditation means to sit there with one hundred percent of yourself. If at first you are there with only eighty percent, that is good enough. You will get better and better all the time. Maybe yesterday it was eighty percent, but today it may be eighty-one percent. The more present you are, the happier and more solid you become. Sitting is only for your happiness and stability, not for someone else's.

When we sit and meditate, we stop and let our mind become calm and clear. It's like mud settling in water. If you put mud into a glass of water and let it sit, the mud will slowly settle to the bottom of the glass and the water will become clear. If you stir the mud around, it will not have a chance to settle. When the mud is calm, the water is clear. The same is true of your mind.

When you sit, feel free to sit in any position—the lotus, half-lotus, or the chrysanthemum position. The lotus position is the cross-legged position with both feet resting on top of the opposite thigh. The chrysanthemum position is whatever position you like. Choose the position that is most comfortable for you. The lotus position is considered by many to be the most beautiful and stable position. If I sit in this position, then my body is very stable; even if you push me, I will not fall over. When our body is stable, it's easier for our mind to be stable too, because body and mind influence each other.

Can meditation affect our unhappiness? Yes, it can. Through meditation, happiness becomes more available and unhappiness begins to diminish. Through meditation, our garbage is transformed into compost so it can soon become flowers again. Through meditation, we learn to practice being happy and making other people happy. This is how we take care of our unhappiness.

Planting Seeds of Happiness

You have both seeds of happiness and unhappiness in you, planted by your parents, your ancestors, or your friends. When seeds of happiness manifest themselves, you feel quite happy. But when seeds of sorrow, anger, and hatred manifest, you feel very unhappy. The quality of our life depends on what seeds we water in our consciousness.

When you practice breathing, smiling, and looking at the beautiful things around you, you are planting seeds of beauty and happiness. That is why we practice things like breathing in and seeing ourselves as a flower, breathing out and feeling fresh; breathing in and seeing ourselves as a mountain, breathing out and feeling solid like a mountain. This practice helps us plant seeds of solidity and freshness in ourselves. Every time we walk with calm and ease, or we smile and release the tension in us, we are planting seeds that will strengthen our happiness. With each happy step, we plant a happy seed.

Happiness cannot be separated from suffering. We know happiness because we know suffering. If we haven't experienced hunger, we can't fully realize how happy we can be when we have something to eat. If we haven't lived the life of a homeless person, we won't appreciate fully the fact that we have a home to live in. That is why happiness cannot be separated from suffering. It means that if you have suffered, you can be happy. If you do not know anything about suffering, you cannot be a happy person.

You Have Never Been Born

When you look at the sheet of paper you are reading from, you may think that it did not exist before it was made at the paper mill. But there is a cloud floating in this sheet of paper. If there were no cloud, there could be no rain, and therefore no tree could grow to give us this piece of paper. If you remove the cloud from the paper, the paper will collapse. If you are a poet—and even if you are not a poet—you can see a cloud floating in this piece of paper. Looking deeply into the sheet of paper, and touching it deeply, you can also touch the cloud.

Shall we ask whether this paper existed before it was born? Has it come from nothing? No, something never comes from nothing. The sheet of paper "inter-is" with the sunshine, with the rain, with the earth, with the paper factory, with the workers in the factory, with the food that the workers eat every day. So the nature of the paper is inter-being. If you touch the paper, you touch everything in the cosmos. Before its birth in the factory, the paper was the sunshine, it was a tree.

You may also think that when you were born, you suddenly became something and that before you had been nothing; that from being no one, you suddenly became someone. But actually, the moment of your birth in the hospital or at home was just a moment of continuation, because you had already existed in your mother for nine months. That means your birth date on your birth certificate is not correct; you have to push it back nine months earlier.

So now perhaps you believe that you have the truth; that the moment of your conception is the moment when you began to exist. But we should continue to look deeply. Before the moment of conception, were you a nothing, a no one? No. Before that, half of you was in your father, and the other half was in your mother, in another form. That is why even the moment of conception is a moment of continuation.

Imagine the ocean with its multitude of waves. The waves are all different; some are big, some are small, some are more beautiful than others. You can describe waves in many ways, but when you touch a wave, you are always touching something else—water.

Visualize yourself as a wave on the surface of the ocean. Watch as you are being created: you rise to the surface, you stay a little while, and then you return to the ocean. You know that at some point you are going to end. But if you know how to touch the ground of your being—water—all your fears will vanish. You will see that as a wave, you share the life of the water with every other wave. This is the nature of our interbeing. When we live only the life of a wave and are not able to live the life of water, we suffer quite a lot.

So if you define birth as becoming something from nothing, becoming someone from no one, then you have never been born. But the reality is, every moment is a moment of continuation. You continue life in new forms, that's all.

When a cloud is about to become rain, it's not scared, because although it knows that to be a cloud floating in the sky is wonderful, to be the rain falling down on the fields and oceans is also wonderful. That is why the moment a cloud becomes rain is not a moment of death, but a moment of continuation.

There are people who think that they can reduce things into nothingness. They think they can eliminate people, that they can kill someone like John F. Kennedy, Martin Luther King, Jr., or Mahatma Gandhi, with the hope that they will disappear forever. But the fact is that when you kill someone, that person becomes stronger than before. Even this sheet of paper cannot be reduced to nothing. You have seen what happens when you put a match to a piece of paper. It doesn't become nothing; it continues on as heat, ashes, and smoke.

Buddha and Mara

When we talk about what a Buddha is, we also have to talk about what a Buddha isn't. The opposite of the Buddha is Mara. If the Buddha is enlightenment, then there has to be something that isn't enlightenment. Mara is the absence of enlightenment. If the Buddha is understanding, then Mara is misunderstanding, and if the Buddha is loving kindness, then Mara is hatred or anger, and so on. If we don't understand Mara, we can't understand the Buddha.

Just as a rose is made of non-rose elements, the Buddha is made of non-Buddha elements, and among those elements is Mara. If the garbage doesn't exist, then the rose doesn't exist either. This insight is so important; it completely transformed my understanding of the Buddha.

When you look at a rose, you may see the rose as very pure and beautiful. And the opposite of a rose is garbage, which is not beautiful and does not smell very good. But if you look deeply at the rose, you will see that the garbage is in there—before, after, and also right now while the rose is still blooming. How is this possible?

Good organic gardeners don't throw away garbage. They know that with care, in just a few months, the garbage will become compost that can then be used to grow lettuce, tomatoes, and flowers. Gardeners are capable of seeing flowers or cucumbers in the garbage. Yet, they also know that all flowers become garbage. That is the meaning of impermanence—all the flowers have to become garbage. Although garbage stinks and is unpleasant, if you know how to take care of it, you can transform it back into flowers. That's what the Buddha described as the nondualistic way of looking at things. If you look at things in this way, you will understand that the garbage is capable of becoming a flower, and the flower is capable of becoming garbage.

Every time you practice mindfulness, and when you live mindfully, you are Buddha. When you live in forgetfulness, you are Mara. But don't think that the Buddha and Mara are enemies that spend all day fighting with each other. No. They are friends. Here is a story that I wrote.

One day, the Buddha was staying in a cave, where it was cool. Ananda, the Buddha's attendant, was practicing walking meditation near the cave, trying to intercept the many people who always came to visit the Buddha so that the Buddha wouldn't have to receive guests all day long. That day, as Ananda was practicing, he saw someone approaching. As the person drew near, Ananda recognized Mara.

Mara had tried to tempt the Buddha the night before the Buddha became enlightened. Mara had told the Buddha that he could become a man of great power—a politician, a king, a president, a government minister, or a successful businessman with money and beautiful women—if he gave up his mindfulness practice. Mara had tried very hard to convince the Buddha, but it hadn't worked.

Although Ananda felt very uncomfortable at the sight of Mara, Mara had already seen him, so he couldn't hide. They greeted each other. Mara said, "I want to see the Buddha."

When the head of a corporation doesn't want to see someone, she asks her secretary to say, "I'm sorry, she's in a conference now." Even though Ananda wanted to say something like that, he knew it would be lying and he wanted to practice the fourth precept of no lying. So he decided to say to Mara what was in his heart.

"Mara, why should the Buddha see you? What is the purpose? Don't you remember how you were defeated by the Buddha under the Bodhi tree? How can you bear to see him again? Have you no shame? Why should he see you? You are his enemy."

Mara was not discouraged by the Venerable Ananda's words. He just smiled as he listened to the young monk. When Ananda had finished, Mara laughed and asked, "Did your teacher really say that he has enemies?"

This made Ananda very uncomfortable. It didn't seem right for him to say that the Buddha had enemies, but he had said it! The Buddha had never said that he had enemies. If you are not practicing mindfulness and concentration, you may say things that are contrary to what you know to be so. Ananda was confused. He went into the cave to announce Mara, hoping that his teacher would say, "Tell him I'm not at home!" or, "Tell him I'm in a conference!"

To Ananda's surprise, the Buddha smiled and said, "Mara! Wonderful! Ask him to come in!" Ananda was baffled by this response from the Buddha. But he did as the Buddha said and invited Mara in. And you know what the Buddha did? He hugged Mara! Ananda could not understand this. Then the Buddha invited Mara to sit in the best spot in the cave, and turning to his beloved disciple he said, "Ananda, would you like to go and make some herb tea for us?"

As you may have guessed, Ananda was not very happy about this. Making tea for the Buddha was one thing—he could do that a thousand times a day—but making tea for Mara was not something he wanted to do. But since the Buddha had asked him to do it, he could not refuse.

Buddha looked at Mara lovingly. "Dear friend," he said, "how have you been? Is everything okay?"

Mara replied, "No, things are not okay at all, they

are very bad. I'm very tired of being Mara. I want to be someone else, someone like you. Wherever you go you are welcome, and people bow before you. You have many monks and nuns with lovely faces following you, and you are given offerings of bananas, oranges, and kiwis.

"Everywhere I go," Mara continued, "I have to wear the persona of a Mara—I have to speak in a convincing manner and keep an army of wicked little Maras. Every time I breathe out, I have to blow smoke from my nose! But I don't even mind these things so much; what bothers me more is that my disciples, the little Maras, have begun to talk about transformation and healing. When they talk about liberation and Buddhahood, I can't bear it. That is why I have come to ask you if we can exchange roles. You can be a Mara, and I'll be a Buddha."

When the Venerable Ananda heard this, it frightened him so much he thought his heart would stop. What if the Buddha decided to exchange roles? Then Ananda would have to be Mara's attendant! Ananda hoped the Buddha would refuse.

The Buddha calmly looked at Mara and smiled. "Do you think it is easy to be Buddha?" he asked. "People are always misunderstanding me and putting words into my mouth. They build temples with statues of me made from copper, plaster, gold, or even emerald. Large crowds of people offer me bananas, oranges, sweets, and other things. Sometimes they carry a statue of me in a procession, looking like a drunk person sitting on heaps of flowers. I don't like being this kind of a Buddha. So many harmful things have been done in my name. So you can see that being a Buddha is also very difficult. Being a teacher and helping people practice is not an easy job. In fact, I don't think you'd enjoy being a Buddha very much. It is better if we both continue doing what we are doing and try to make the best of it."

If you had been there with Ananda, and if you had been very mindful, you might have felt that Buddha and Mara were friends. They meet each other like day and night, like flower and garbage coming together. This is a very deep teaching of the Buddha.

Now you have an idea of what kind of relationship exists between Buddha and Mara. Buddha is like a flower, very fresh and beautiful. Mara is like garbage, smelly, covered with flies, and unpleasant to touch. Mara is not at all pleasant, but if you know how to help transform Mara, Mara will become Buddha. And if you don't know how to take care of the Buddha, Buddha will become Mara.

Looking at things in this way, we know that the non-rose elements, including the garbage, have come together in order to make the rose possible. So the Buddha is something like a rose. But if you look deeply into the Buddha, you see Mara; Buddha is made of Mara elements. And when you understand this Buddhist teaching, you see the emptiness of everything, because nothing has its own absolute existence. A rose is made of non-rose elements, so it has no separate existence; that is why it is called "empty." A rose is empty of a separate self, because it is always made of non-rose elements.

Interbeing includes everything, not only Buddha and Mara, roses and garbage, but also suffering and happiness, good and evil. Take suffering, for instance. Suffering is made of happiness, and happiness is made of suffering. Good is made of evil, and evil is made of good. Right is made of left, and left is made of right. This needs that in order to be. Removing this, that will disappear. The Buddha said, "This is, because that is." This is a very special and important teaching of Buddhism.

So the practice of Buddhist meditation begins with the acceptance of the rose and the garbage in us. When we see the rose in us, we're happy, but we are aware that if we don't take good care of it, it will quickly become a piece of garbage. Therefore, we learn how to take care of the rose so that it will stay with us longer. When it begins to deteriorate into garbage, we are not afraid, because we know how to transform the garbage into the rose again. So when you witness a feeling of distress, if you look deeply into that feeling, you will see a tiny seed of happiness and liberation in it. That is how transformation takes place.

Like Leaves on a Banana Tree

One day I was contemplating a young banana tree. I took the banana tree as the subject of my meditation, my mindfulness and concentration. This was a very young banana tree with only three leaves. First, there was a big sister leaf, then a second sister leaf. The third and youngest leaf was still curled up inside.

When I looked at these banana leaves deeply, I saw that the big sister had her own life to live. She unfurled herself, enjoying the sunshine and the rain, and she was a very beautiful leaf. She gave the impression that she only cared about herself. But if you looked deeply, you could see something entirely different. Because while she enjoyed her life as the first leaf, she was helping the second and third leaves, and even a fourth leaf that was not yet visible but had already formed inside the trunk of the banana tree. She was doing the work of nourishing the whole banana tree.

Each minute of her life, this first leaf practiced breathing and smiling. She transformed the nutrients that she received through the roots of the banana tree into nourishment for herself. She then sent this nourishment back to the tree and all her younger sisters and sisters-to-be. She lived her own life and yet her life had meaning; she was helping to nourish and raise future generations.

The second leaf was doing exactly the same thing. She lived her life as a leaf fully, but she also did the work of teaching, nourishing, and bringing up her younger sisters. But if you did not look deeply, you would not see that the first and second leaves were doing the same thing at the same time. The third leaf, though the youngest, would in no time at all be unfurling herself, too. She would soon become a beautiful leaf and take care of her younger sisters.

The same is true for you. By living your life beautifully, you can nourish your sisters, your brothers, and future generations. It is not through sacrificing your life that you help future generations; it is by living your life fully and happily.

When young people say, "I have my own life to live," or "This body is mine, and I can do whatever I like with it," this is not reality. It is a misconception. We are not separate from each other. Your body is not just yours, it belongs to your ancestors, your grandparents, and your parents. It also belongs to your children and grandchildren who are not yet born, but who are already present in your body.

You and your parents are one reality. If your parents suffer, you suffer. If you suffer, your parents suffer. If we look deeply and see clearly, we will see that there is just one reality. When you look in that way, you will see clearly that happiness is collective, and you will not go looking for your own individual happiness anymore. You will see that we have to work together and understand one another.

The Two Promises

I often suggest to young people that they take two vows:

1) I vow to develop understanding in order to live peacefully with people, animals, plants, and minerals.
2) I vow to develop compassion in order to protect the lives of people, animals, plants, and minerals.

In order to love, you need to understand, because love is made of understanding. If you do not understand someone, you cannot love him or her. Meditation is looking deeply to understand the needs and suffering of the other person. When you feel that you are understood, you feel love penetrating you. It's a wonderful feeling. All of us need understanding and love.

People like doing different things. Suppose your friend wants to play tennis after school, and you want to read a book. But because you want to make your friend happy, you put down your book and go out to play tennis with him. You are practicing understanding when you do this. Through your understanding, you give your friend joy.

When you make him happy, you become happy, too. This is an example of practicing understanding and loving.

Whenever you recite these two vows, ask yourself these questions: "Since I have made these vows, have I tried to learn about them? Have I tried to practice the vows?" I do not expect a yes or no answer to these questions. Even if you have tried to learn about the vows and have tried to practice them, it is not enough. The best way to respond to these questions is to open yourself and let the questions enter deeply into your whole being while you breathe in and out. Just by opening yourself up to the questions and letting them enter, they will begin to work silently.

Understanding and love are the two most important teachings of the Buddha. If we do not make an effort to be open, to understand the suffering of other people, we will not be able to love them and live in harmony with them. We should also try to understand and protect the lives of animals, plants, and minerals, and live in harmony with them. If we can't understand, we can't love. The Buddha teaches us to look at living beings with the eyes of love and understanding. Please learn to practice this teaching.

Chasing Clouds

What is true happiness? Often we think that we cannot be happy if we don't get what we want. There are a million ways to be happy, but because we don't know how to open the door to happiness, we just chase after the things we think we want. The truth is, the more you chase after happiness, the more you suffer.

I have a nice story to tell you about a stream that descended from a mountaintop. The stream was very young, and her goal was to reach the ocean. She only wanted to run as quickly as possible. But when she got down to the plains, to the lowlands and the fields below, she slowed down; she became a river. A river cannot run as quickly as a young stream of water.

Flowing slowly along, she began to reflect the clouds in the sky. There were many kinds of clouds with many different forms and colors. Soon the river was spending all of her time chasing clouds, one after another. But the clouds would not stand still, they came and went, and she chased after them. When the river saw that no cloud wanted to stay with her, it made her very sad, and she cried.

One day, there was a strong wind that blew all the clouds

away. The sky was magnificently blue. But because there were no clouds, the river began to think that life was not worth living anymore. She did not know how to enjoy the blue sky. She found the sky empty, and her life, too, seemed to have lost its meaning.

That night, her despair was so great that she wanted to die. But how can a river die? From being someone you can't become no one; from being something, you can't become nothing. All night long, the river cried, her tears lapping against the shore. That was the first time she had gone back to herself. Before that, she had always run away from herself. Instead of looking for happiness inside, she had looked for it on the outside. So the first time she went back to herself and listened to the sound of her tears, she discovered something startling: she realized that she was, in fact, made of clouds.

It was strange. She had been chasing after clouds, thinking that she could not be happy without clouds, yet she herself was made of clouds. What she was seeking was already in her.

Happiness can be like that. If you know how to go back to the here and now, you will realize that the elements of your happiness are already available to you. You don't need to chase them anymore.

Suddenly, the river became aware of something reflecting on her cool, still surface. It was the blue sky. How peaceful, how free was that beautiful blue sky. This filled her with happiness. She was able to reflect the sky for the first time. Before that, she had only reflected the clouds and chased after them. She had completely ignored the presence of the intense, blue sky that was always available to her. She hadn't noticed that her happiness was made of the solidity, freedom, and space that were already there. That was a night of deep transformation, and her tears and suffering were transformed into joy and peace.

The next morning, the wind came up and the clouds returned. Now the river found that she could reflect the clouds with no attachment, with equanimity. Every time a cloud came, she said, "Hello, cloud." And when the cloud left, she was not sad at all and told it, "I will see you sometime later." She knew now that her freedom was the very foundation of her happiness. She had learned to stop and to not run anymore.

Then one night, something wonderful revealed itself to her: the image of the full moon reflected on her surface. It made her very happy. Holding hands with the clouds and the moon, she now made her way towards the ocean—but she was no longer in a hurry to reach it, she was enjoying every moment. Each of us is a river.

Practices

✳

Touching the Buddha Inside

In Buddhist texts, called "sutras," the most important message is that everyone has the capacity to be a Buddha—the capacity to love, understand, and be enlightened. This is the most important message from all the sutras.

The practice I would like to show you is called "Recollection of the Buddha," and it is taught in every school of Buddhism. You touch the Buddha and all the qualities of the Buddha inside you, and you know that the Buddha is absolutely real—not an idea or a notion, but a reality. Our task, our life, our practice is to nourish the Buddha in us and in the people we love.

You may like to spend three or four minutes on this practice, either alone or together with a few friends. Sit down quietly, breathe in and out for a few minutes to calm yourself, and then ask, "Little Buddha, are you there?" Ask the question very deeply and quietly. "My little Buddha, are you there?" In the beginning, you might not hear an answer. There is always an answer, but if you are not calm enough, you won't hear it. "Anyone there? Little Buddha, are you there?" And then you will hear the voice of your little Buddha answering, "Yes, my dear, of course. I am always here for you."

Hearing this, you smile. "I know, little Buddha, you are my calm. I know you are always there, and I need you to help me be calm. Often, I am not as calm as I'd like to be. I shout, I act as if I don't have a Buddha in me. But because I know you are there, I know I am capable of being calm. Thank you, little Buddha, I need you to be there." And the little Buddha says, "Of course I'll be here for you all the time. Just come and visit me whenever you need to." That is the practice of touching the Buddha inside. It's a very important practice for all of us.

I love to sit close to children because of their freshness. Every time I hold the hand of a child and practice walking meditation, I benefit from his or her freshness. I can offer the child my stability, and from the child I always receive his or her freshness. If you lose your peace and joy, remember that you have been fresh many times in the past. And if you touch the Buddha, the freshness in you will continue to grow.

You can say to the Buddha inside of you, "Dear little Buddha, you are my freshness. Thank you for being there."

"Dear little Buddha, you are my tenderness." Tenderness is what all of us need.

"Dear little Buddha, you are my mindfulness." And that is true, because a Buddha is someone who is made of the energy of mindfulness. To be mindful means to be aware of what is happening, and that is only possible when you are really there, one hundred percent. Whenever you act mindfully—whether you are drinking a glass of juice, walking, or breathing mindfully—you are touching your own Buddhahood, your Buddha nature.

"Dear Buddha, you are my understanding." Understanding is so crucial. If you don't understand someone, you cannot love him or her. When you are mindful and aware of everything that is going on inside you and around you, you understand things and people very easily. So you can say, "Little Buddha, you are my understanding. I need you very much because I know that understanding is the foundation of love."

"Dear little Buddha, you are my capacity of loving." You, too, have the capacity to love. If you touch that capacity every day, your love will grow and you will be on your way to fully realizing the Buddha within yourself.

Every time you visit the Buddha, the Buddha in you will grow stronger. The Buddha in you will have more space and air to breathe. During the day, you may have suffered, you may have been very angry, your little Buddha may be suffocating. But every time you practice touching the Buddha, you bring in a lot of space and air, and the Buddha within you has a chance to grow. It's very important.

If you practice touching these qualities of the Buddha in you, you are touching the real Buddha, not the Buddha made of plaster, copper, or even emeralds. The Buddha is not a statue. The Buddha is not a god. The Buddha is not someone outside of us, up in the sky or on a mountaintop. The Buddha is alive and living in us.

"Dear Buddha, it is very comforting to know that you are there. Little Buddha, I need you very much." And the little Buddha in you will say, "Dear one, I also need you very much. Please come and visit more often."

Eating an Orange

When you look deeply at an orange, you realize that an orange—or any fruit —is nothing less than a miracle. Try it. Take an orange and hold it in your palm. Breathe in and out slowly, and look at it as if you were seeing it for the first time.

When you look at it deeply, you will be able to see many wonderful things—the sun shining and the rain falling on the orange tree, the orange blossoms, the tiny fruit appearing on the branch, the color of the fruit changing from green to yellow, and then the full-grown orange. Now slowly begin to peel it. Smell the wonderful scent of the orange peel. Break off a section of the orange and put it into your mouth. Taste its wonderful juice.

The orange tree has taken three, four, or six months to make such an orange for you. It is a miracle. Now the orange is ready and it says, "I am here for you." But if you are not present, you will not hear it. When you are not looking at the orange in the present moment, then the orange is not present either.

Being fully present while eating an orange, an ice cream cone, or any other food is a delightful experience.

Mindful Eating

Eating in mindfulness is a deep and joyful practice. Before we eat our meal, we can practice breathing mindfully and looking deeply at the food on the table. As we breathe in and out we can notice the sunshine, the wheat field, and the clouds that have brought us the wonderful food that we eat today. We have a practice of reciting contemplations before we eat our food. They help us to be really mindful of the food and enjoy it more deeply. We have a version for young people that goes like this:

* This food is the gift of the whole universe: The earth, the sky, the rain, and the sun.
* We thank the people who have made this food, especially the farmers, the people at the market, and the cooks.
* We only put on our plate as much food as we can eat.
* We want to chew the food slowly so that we can enjoy it.

✳ This food gives us energy to practice being more
loving and understanding.

✳ We eat this food in order to be healthy and happy,
and to love each other as a family.

Tree-hugging

When you touch a tree, you receive something beautiful and refreshing back. Trees are wonderful! They are also solid, even in a storm. We can learn a lot from trees.

Find a tree that is especially beautiful to you—perhaps it's an apple tree, an oak tree, or a pine tree. If you stop and touch a tree deeply, you will feel its wonderful qualities. Breathing deeply will help you touch the tree deeply. Breathe in, touch the tree, then breathe out. Do this three times. Touching the tree in this way will make you feel refreshed and happy.

Then, if you like, you can hug the tree. Tree-hugging is a wonderful practice. When you hug a tree, a tree never refuses. You can rely on a tree. It is dependable. Every time you want to see it, every time you need its shade, it is there for you.

In my home in Plum Village, I planted three cedar trees. I planted them about thirty years ago, and now they are very big and beautiful, and very refreshing. While I am doing walking meditation, I usually stop in front of one of the trees. I bow to it. It makes me feel happy. I touch the bark with my cheek. I smell the tree. I look up at the beautiful leaves. I feel the strength and freshness of the tree. I breathe in and out deeply. It's very pleasant, and sometimes I stay for a long time, just enjoying the lovely tree.

Touching the Earth

In Plum Village we do a practice called "Touching the Earth" every day. It helps us in many ways. You, too, could be helped by doing this practice. When you feel restless or lack confidence in yourself, or when you feel angry or unhappy, you can kneel down and touch the earth deeply with your hand. Touch the earth as if it were your favorite thing or your best friend.

The earth has been there for a long time. She is mother to all of us. She knows everything. The Buddha asked the earth to be his witness by touching her with his hand when he had some doubt and fear before his awakening. The earth appeared to him as a beautiful mother. In her arms she carried flowers and fruit, birds and butterflies, and many different animals and offered them to the Buddha. The Buddha's doubts and fears instantly disappeared.

Whenever you feel unhappy, come to the earth and ask for her help. Touch her deeply, the way the Buddha did. Suddenly, you too will see the earth with all her flowers and fruit, trees and birds, animals, and all the living beings that she has produced. All these things she offers to you.

You have more opportunities to be happy than you ever

thought. The earth shows her love to you, and her patience. The earth is very patient. She sees you suffer, she helps you, she protects you. When we die, she takes us back into her arms.

With the earth you are very safe. She is always there, in all her wonderful expressions like trees, flowers, butter-flies, and sunshine. Whenever you are tired or unhappy, touching the earth is a very good practice to heal you and restore your joy.

Breathing Meditation

W hen I breathe in, I know that I am breathing in. The "I know" is very important. Your breath is the link between your body and your mind. It's so nice when you are in touch with that link; then you are in touch with everything in yourself, body and mind. And right away, you are master of yourself in any situation. You are not carried away by anybody or anything, including your thoughts. Your mind is fully with your body and your whole being. When you start to know that you are breathing in or that you are breathing out, you start to know what you are doing—whether you are sitting, standing, or walking. So knowing, being aware, is very important.

Don't think that practicing Buddhism is very difficult. It's not difficult; it's easy. Can you breathe in and out and know that you are breathing in and out? Breathing in and breathing out—that is mindfulness. First, practice being mindful of your breath; then of your body; then of your mind; and then of everything around you.

Conscious breathing is a very good practice. In our daily life, if we don't know how to breathe mindfully, and how to stop our thinking, we cannot get in touch with the wonderful things in life like the sunshine, rivers, clouds, our family, and our friends. So being aware of our breathing is very important.

Mindful breathing is easy to practice, and very enjoyable. Here is a gatha that you can say to yourself as you sit for a few minutes breathing. Say the first sentence as you breathe in, and the second sentence as you breathe out. As you continue to breathe, you may just want to use the key words, the first one with your in-breath, and the second one with your out-breath:

Breathing in, I know I am breathing in.
Breathing out, I know I am breathing out.
In/Out.

Breathing in, I see myself as a flower.
Breathing out, I feel fresh.
Flower/Fresh.

Breathing in, I see myself as a mountain.
Breathing out, I feel solid.
Mountain/Solid.

Breathing in, I see myself as still water.
Breathing out, I reflect things as they are.
Water/Reflecting.

Breathing in, I see myself as space.
Breathing out, I feel free.
Space/Free.

First, practice "In/Out" three times. "Breathing in, I know I am breathing in. Breathing out, I know I am breathing out." Then move to the exercise called "Flower/Fresh." "Breathing in, I see myself as a flower. Breathing out, I feel fresh."

Then practice "Mountain/Solid." The cross-legged position is a very stable and solid position. If you manage to sit cross-legged, breathing silently and smiling, you will be as solid as a mountain; you will not be blown away by any emotions, thoughts, or winds from any direction. So, "Breathing in, I see myself as a mountain. Breathing out, I feel solid."

Then practice the exercise "Water/Reflecting." Looking at the clear and still lake water, you can see the sky and clouds reflected in the water as clearly as when you look up at the sky and clouds themselves. Have you had this experience? "Breathing in, I see myself as still water. Breathing out, I reflect things as they are." This means that I don't distort things. Don't say, "I feel like still water." Say, "Breathing in, I see myself as still water." We are ourselves the water. We are ourselves the mountain. We are ourselves the flower. I reflect exactly the blue sky that I see.

I don't distort things, because I am clear, I am solid, and I am calm.

Still water is very calm. When you are calm, you reflect reality well. When you are not calm and still, you perceive things incorrectly and distort them. It is like seeing a piece of rope and thinking it's a snake. Because you are not peaceful or calm enough, you don't reflect reality as it is. Have you looked in one of those funny mirrors that distorts images? Looking in those mirrors, you can hardly recognize yourself; your face is long and your eyes are big. Have you had that experience? It is not how you really look.

The last part of the exercise is "Space/Free." "Breathing in, I see myself as space. Breathing out, I feel free." With space, you feel so at ease. When people give you enough space and freedom, you are happier. When you breathe in, you see yourself as infinite space—space in which everything moves freely—and you can breathe. Without that space, you cannot breathe or smile.

When you're empty, it means you're not repressing anything within yourself—no hatred, anger, despair, or craving. As empty space, you feel wonderful. When you breathe out, say, "I feel free." "Breathing in, I see myself as space. Breathing out, I feel free." Try it.

The images of flower, mountain, water, and space will help you have better concentration and feel refreshed, stable, calm, and free.

Sitting Meditation

Another breathing exercise you can practice during your sitting meditation is: "In/Out, Deep/Slow, Calm/Ease, Smile/Release, Present Moment/Wonderful Moment."

Breathing in, I know that I am breathing in.
Breathing out, I know that I am breathing out.

As my in-breath grows deep,
My out-breath grows slow.

Breathing in makes me calm,
Breathing out brings me ease.

With the in-breath, I smile,
With the out-breath, I release.

Dwelling in the present moment,
I know this is a wonderful moment.

"Breathing in, I know that I am breathing in. Breathing out, I know that I am breathing out." That is the first verse. Then, "As my in-breath grows deep, my out-breath grows slow." You recognize the quality of your breath as it is now. You don't want to make it long or deep, you just recognize it as it is. And as you maintain awareness of your breath, you'll notice that it naturally becomes deeper and slower. After doing that a few times, you move to "Calm/Ease."

"Breathing in makes me calm. Breathing out brings me ease." Ease is like space, it is the feeling of being light and free. You cannot be happy unless you are light and free. Ease means that you do not take anything too seriously; nothing is more important than your peace.

"With the in-breath, I smile." Why smile? You smile because you feel at ease. And when you smile, all the muscles on your can face relax. You're able to see what is important and what is not important. "With the out-breath, I release." You are able to smile at the unimportant things and let them go. This is release. Release is the source of happiness.

"Dwelling in the present moment, I know this is a wonderful moment." You need only to allow yourself to be in the present moment and you will be able to touch many, many conditions of happiness.

The practice is easy. Peace and happiness are there to some extent, along with pain and suffering. But remember, like watching television, you are free to select from the channels made available to you. You can choose peace and happiness.

Flower Arranging

We arrange flowers because we want life to be beautiful. When we know how to arrange flowers, then we know how to be with ourselves and with the people around us because we are all flowers. As we arrange flowers, we arrange ourselves.

To make a flower arrangement, first you need to find a flower. Perhaps there is a garden or a field where you can pick a flower. When you pick a flower, you can show your appreciation for its presence, for its beauty, by saying "thank you" and smiling to it. Do this before picking it and also after picking it. Put it in a container of fresh water immediately so that it will be nourished right away.

You might think that you need many flowers to make a flower arrangement. But in fact, even without flowers, you can make beautiful arrangements. All you need is a branch from the ground, dry leaves, a rock, a feather, or some sand. Thank them as you thanked the flower, and sit down and start arranging them.

Arrange the things you have chosen in such a way that there is peace and harmony among them. If you breathe and smile while you are arranging them, the feeling of peace inside of you and inside the arrangement grows. But if you just throw the various items together without care, when you step back and look, you won't see peace because the different pieces are fighting each other.

When you arrange flowers, you also arrange the space in between and around the flowers and other items. Space between flowers creates a sense of freedom in us and in the hearts of people looking at the arrangement.

Flower arranging takes time. There's no need to hurry. Rushing defeats your purpose. Allow yourself enough time so that you stay very present during the process. That way, your flower arranging will create beauty and peace and will be enjoyable to you and everyone else.

After you have finished your flower arrangement, you might want to give it a name and say it out loud. You can draw a picture of your creation and write its name. You can send your drawing to me in Plum Village, if you like.

Pebble Meditation

I don't carry a credit card, money, or cigarettes in my pocket. Instead, there may be a sheet of paper or a little bell. I usually like to carry a few pebbles. These pebbles help remind me that we humans are born as flowers in the garden of humanity; if we don't know how to preserve our freshness, then we suffer and we do not have enough beauty to offer to the person we love.

This Pebble Meditation came from a retreat for children that we had over twenty years ago. About 300 children and their parents came and together we invented this way to remind ourselves of the freshness and flower-like elements in everyone.

Make a little bag, and into it put four pebbles that you have collected outside. You can sit in a circle with other children or with members of your family, and one child or person in the family plays the role of bell master. After having invited the bell to sound three times and enjoying breathing in and breathing out, pour the pebbles out of the bag and set them on the ground to your left.

With your right hand, pick up one pebble and look at it.

The first pebble represents a flower. It also represents your own freshness and flower nature. Put the pebble on the palm of your left hand, and put the left hand on the right hand to begin your meditation on flower nature:

Breathing in, I see myself as a flower.
Breathing out, I feel fresh.

That is not imagination, because you are a flower in the garden of humanity. See yourself as a flower. It is very helpful to smile during the practice, because a flower is always smiling. Practice this meditation three times. After that, put the pebble down on the ground to your right.

Then pick up the second pebble and look at it. This pebble represents a mountain. A mountain represents solidity. You are yourself, you are stable, and you are solid. Without solidity, you can't be truly happy. You will be pulled away by provocations, anger, fear, regret, or anxiety. This meditation is best practiced in the sitting position because in the half lotus or lotus position your body feels very stable and solid. Even if someone comes and pushes you, you will not fall. After you place the second pebble in your left hand, begin to meditate on the mountain.

Breathing in, I see myself as a mountain.
Breathing out, I feel solid.

Repeat this three times. When you are solid, you are no longer shaky in your body and in your mind.

The third pebble represents still water. From time to time, you see a lake where the water is so still that it reflects exactly what is there. It's so still it can reflect the blue sky, the white clouds, the mountains, the trees. You can aim your camera at the lake and take a picture of the sky and the mountain reflected there just the same. When your mind is calm, it reflects things as they are. You aren't a victim of wrong perceptions. When your mind is disturbed by craving, anger, or jealousy, you perceive things wrongly. Wrong perceptions bring us a lot of anger, fear, violence, and push us to do or to say things that will destroy everything. This practice helps you restore your calm and peace, represented by still water.

Breathing in, I see myself as still water.
Breathing out, I reflect things as they truly are.

Repeat this three times. This is not wishful thinking. With mindful breathing, you can bring peace to your breath, body, and feelings.

The fourth pebble represents space and freedom. If you do not have enough space in your heart, it will be very difficult for you to feel happy. If you are arranging flowers, you understand that flowers need space around to radiate their beauty. Each person needs some space as well. If you love someone, one of the most precious things you can offer him is space. And this you can't buy in the supermarket. Visualize the moon sailing in the sky. The moon has a lot of space around it, that is part of its beauty. Many of the disciples of the Buddha described him as a full moon sailing in the empty sky.

Breathing in, I see myself as space.
Breathing out, I feel free.

Repeat this three times. Each person needs freedom and space. Offer space to the loved ones in your family as well. Without imposing your ideas or ways on the other person, you can offer them the gift of this pebble meditation. In this way, it is possible for you to help remove the worries, fears, and anger in the heart of each person in your family.

Walking Meditation

While you are walking, smile—be in the here and the now. By doing so, you transform the place where you are walking into paradise. Walk slowly. Don't rush. Each step brings you to the best moment of your life, the present moment.

If you say the following gatha to yourself while you walk, your walk will be even more enjoyable:

Breathing in, I know I am breathing in.
Breathing out, I know I am breathing out.

As my in-breath grows deep,
My out-breath grows slow.

Breathing in, I calm my body,
Breathing out, I feel at ease.

Breathing in, I smile,
Breathing out, I release.

Dwelling in the present moment,
I know this is a wonderful moment.

As you continue walking and breathing, you can shorten the gatha to: in/out, deep/slow, calm/ease, smile/release, present moment/wonderful moment.

Yes, Thanks

Saying "Yes, thanks" is a wonderful way to do walking meditation.

During the in-breath, you can take two steps and say, "Yes, yes." During the out-breath, take two steps and say, "Thanks, thanks."

We can all practice saying "Yes," as sometimes we are too accustomed to saying "No." Learn to say "Yes" to the blue sky, to the light of the sun, to the beautiful planet Earth, to the birds, to the trees. There are many wonderful things around us, including our father and our mother. We are very lucky to have the blue sky, the clean air, the limpid water, and our parents. When we say "Yes," we recognize that we are lucky, and already this can bring us much happiness.

When you say "Thanks," you are full of gratitude, which is a beautiful thing. Take the hand of your father, your mother, or an uncle or aunt, and practice "Yes, thanks" for just five minutes. Afterward, if you wish, you can run and play. I am sure that if you practice well during these five minutes, you will have a lot of peace and joy.

Four Mantras

A mantra is a magic formula. Every time you pronounce a mantra, you can transform a situation right away; you don't have to wait. You learn it first, and then you can recite it when the time is appropriate. The mantra can only be recited when you're mindful and concentrated. Otherwise it won't work. Because a mantra is not just a statement; it's something you utter because you are in touch with reality. That means you have to be there one hundred percent so that what you say becomes a true mantra.

So before you recite a mantra, breathe in and out and say to yourself: "Breathing in, I am calm, breathing out, I smile. Breathing in, I'm really here, breathing out, I'm really here." Then, when you have done that a few times and feel really there, you can go in the direction of the person you love, look at him or her mindfully, smile, and say the mantra.

The first mantra is, "Darling, I am here for you." When you love someone, you want to offer him or her the best you have. The best thing that you have to offer a loved one is your true presence. This true presence is very important to the other person.

I know a young boy around eleven years old. The boy wasn't very happy, not because he didn't have many things to play with, but because his father was always busy and never spent enough time at home.

One day his father said, "Tomorrow will be your birthday. What would you like? I'll buy it for you." This didn't make the boy very excited. His father was a very rich man and he could afford to buy anything the boy wanted. But what the boy wanted and needed the most was the presence of his father. When someone is rich, she or he has to work very hard in order to continue to be rich; that's the problem. Once you're rich, you can't afford to be poor. So you have to use all your time and energy to work, work, work, day and night, in order to keep being rich. I've seen many people like that father who didn't have time for his child.

The boy didn't know what to say. But he sat with it and then he knew. He said, "Daddy, I know what I want."

"What?" replied his father. He thought his son would say an electric train or something like that. But the boy said, "I want you!" This isn't just true for the boy. What most of us want the most is the presence of the person we love. When the father heard this, he stopped. He was able to really notice his son standing there before him and to be there for him.

The second mantra is, "Darling, I know you are there and I am very happy." This is a very easy mantra to practice. To love means to acknowledge the presence of the person you love and to say that you are very happy that she or he is still alive, available to you at any time. To be able to acknowledge that person, you have to have the time. If you're too busy, how can you acknowledge his or her presence?

The most important condition for saying this mantra is that you are there one hundred percent. If you're not there one hundred percent, you can't recognize his or her presence. When you're loved by someone, you need that person to recognize that you are there. Whether you are very young, or you are eighty or one hundred years old, you still feel the same way. We always need the other person to acknowledge that we are here. We want to be embraced by his or her attention. All of us, children and adults alike, need to be embraced by the energy of mindfulness of our loved ones.

If you are shy, you can go to your room by yourself and try to practice this mantra. Then, when you are sure that you can do it, you can open the door and go to your loved one and practice. I practice these mantras not only with people, but with the moon, the morning star, and the magnolia flowers as well. Some years ago I went to Korea, and I was staying in a Protestant seminary. My little house there was surrounded by magnolias. It was springtime, and the magnolia blossoms were white as snow and very beautiful. I felt so wonderful practicing walking meditation among the magnolia blossoms. I used to stop and look closely at each magnolia flower. I would smile, breathe in and out, and say, "Darling, I know you are there and I am very happy," and I'd bow to the flower. I was very happy, and I thought that the magnolia flower was happy too because when people recognize and appreciate your presence, you feel that you're worth something. The magnolia flowers were very, very precious to me.

Sometimes I look at the full moon with mindfulness, I practice breathing in and out, and I tell the full moon the mantra: "Full moon, beautiful full moon, I know you are there and I am very happy." I am really happy in those moments. I am a free person, not assailed by worries or fear or any projects. Because I am free, I am myself. I have the time and the opportunity to touch the wonders of life around me.

The third mantra is the mantra you practice when you see that the person you love suffers. It is: "Darling, I know you suffer, that's why I am here for you." The person you love may be crying, or if they're not crying, they look very unhappy. Mindfulness helps you to notice that something is wrong within the person you love. The moment you notice that someone you love is suffering, you have to practice deeply in order to be there one hundred percent. Then, you can go to him or her and pronounce the third mantra: "Darling, I know you suffer, that's why I am here for you."

When you suffer, you want the person you love to be aware of your suffering; that's very human. You suffer, and if the other person you love doesn't know that you suffer, then you suffer much more. It is a great relief when our loved ones recognize our suffering. Every time you see your brother or sister suffer, every time you see a friend or parent crying, you can practice. It will bring your loved ones great relief.

The third mantra is to be practiced when the person you love suffers. But the fourth mantra is practiced when you yourself suffer and when you believe that your suffering has been caused by the person you love the most. Because of this, the fourth mantra may seem more difficult at first. With practice it will become easier.

The fourth mantra is: "Darling, I suffer, please help." When the person you love so much says or does something that hurts you, you suffer quite a lot. If another person had said it, you wouldn't have suffered so much. But this is the person you love most in the world and so you can't bear it. You suffer one hundred times more.

According to this practice you have to go to that person, that very person, the person you love the most who just hurt you very deeply, and utter the fourth mantra. When you suffer, and you believe that the person that makes you suffer is the person you love the most, you want to be alone. You want to lock the door to your room and cry alone. You don't want to see him or her. You don't want to talk to him or to her. You don't want to be touched by him or her. "Leave me alone!" you say. This is very normal. Even if the other person tries to approach you and to reconcile, you may still be very angry. You say, "Don't touch me. Leave me alone. I don't want to see you or be with you." That's the real feeling at that moment, very difficult. I think that everyone has had that experience!

But it's possible to practice the fourth mantra. Go to him or her and breathe in deeply and breathe out deeply. Become yourself one hundred percent and just open your mouth and say with all your heart, with all your concentration, that you suffer and you need help. Your pride is deeply hurt. That's why the fourth mantra is so important. In order to be able to practice it, we have to train ourselves for some time.

When you are hurt, you are so sure that your suffering is caused by your loved one, by the one who hurt you. But maybe you are wrong. Maybe he or she hasn't done or said that in order to hurt you but because of his or her own suffering. Perhaps you have a wrong perception. A wrong perception can be the cause of a lot of suffering. And all of us are subject to wrong perceptions every day. That is why whenever we perceive anything, we have to ask ourselves the question, "Are we sure our perception is right?" To be safe, we have to ask.

When we stand with friends looking at the setting sun, we enjoy the beautiful sunset, and we're sure the sun has not set quite yet. But a scientist might tell us that the sun has already set eight minutes ago. The sun we are seeing is only the image of the sun of eight minutes ago. And the scientist is telling the truth, because it takes eight minutes for the image of the sun to come to us; that's the speed of light. But we're very sure that we're seeing the sun setting in the present moment. That is one of our wrong perceptions. We are subject to thousands of wrong perceptions like that in our daily life. It may be that the other person did not have the intention to say or do something to hurt us.

Next time you suffer and you believe that your suffering has been caused by the person you love the most, you have to have already practiced in order to be able to recite the fourth mantra. You have to learn and train yourself now in order to prepare for that time, so that in that moment, you'll be able to practice the fourth mantra. Practice walking meditation, sitting meditation, and breathing in and out mindfully to restore yourself. Then you can go to him or to her and you practice the mantra: "Darling, I suffer so much. You are the person I love most in the world. Please help me." Do it without pride. If you let your pride stand between you and the other person, it means that your love is not really true; because in true love there is no room for pride. If pride is still there, you know that you have to practice in order to transform your love into true love.

The Breathing Room

Every house should have a room called the breathing room, or at least a corner of a room reserved for this purpose. In this place you can put a low table with a flower, a little bell, and enough cushions for everyone in the family to sit on. When you feel uneasy, sad, or angry, you can go into this room, close the door, sit down, invite the sound of the bell, and practice breathing mindfully. When you have breathed like this for ten or fifteen minutes, you begin to feel better. If you do not practice like this, you can lose your temper. Then you may shout or pick a fight with the other person, creating a huge storm in your family.

On one summer retreat at Plum Village, I asked a young boy, "My child, when your father speaks in anger, do you have any way to help your father?" The child shook his head: "I do not know what to do. I become very scared and try to run away." When children come to Plum Village they can learn about the breathing room so they can help their parents when they become angry. I told the young boy, "You can invite your mother or father into your breathing room to breathe with you."

This is something the family must agree about in advance. When everyone is feeling happy, this is a good occasion to ask your father and mother to sign an agreement with each other. You could say: "Daddy, Mommy, sometimes you are angry with each other and say things to hurt each other. This makes me very afraid. Next time this happens, am I allowed to go into the breathing room and invite the sound of the bell to remind you to breathe as our teacher in Plum Village has taught us?" If, at that particular moment, Father and Mother are feeling happy, they will both be very eager to agree. "Of course, my child, next time you see that we are not agreeing, you have the right to go into the breathing room and invite the bell. This will help us remember to breathe together so that we will not make the whole family suffer."

As young children, you are still very fresh. You can use your freshness to help your parents. You can say to your mother, "Mommy, whenever Father says something out of anger that hurts you, you could follow me into the breathing room and we could breathe together instead of arguing with Daddy. What do you think?" If your mother agrees with you, then when your father says something unkind, you go to your mother and take her hand, saying to her, "Let's go into the breathing room, Mommy." When Father sees this, it will wake him up. He will feel admiration for his wife and child because they know how to practice in difficult moments. You can do the same with your father.

Whenever Mother says something unkind to upset Father so that he is about to lose his temper, you can come and take your father's hand, saying quietly, "Daddy, don't be upset. Let's both go into the breathing room."

Once you have gone into the breathing room, you have the sound of the bell and the Buddha to protect you. Everyone in the family can sign an agreement that states: "When we hear the sound of the bell in the breathing room, it is the sound of the Buddha calling us, and everyone in the house will stop and breathe. No one will continue to shout after that." The whole family can make this commitment to stop and breathe at the sound of the bell. This is called "the agreement on living together in peace and joy," which we propose to every family that comes to Plum Village. If you can bring this method of practice home, after about three months you will feel that the atmosphere in the family has become much more pleasant. The wounds in our hearts will be soothed, and gradually they will heal.

The Cake in the Refrigerator

If you have not yet been able to buy a bell or set up a breathing room at your home, you can use a cake. It is a very special cake that I transmit to the children who come to Plum Village so that they can take it home and practice with it. This cake is not made of flour and sugar like a sponge cake. You can keep eating it, and it is never finished. It is called "the cake in the refrigerator."

There will come a day when you are sitting in the living room or dining room and you see that your parents are about to lose their temper with each other. As soon as the atmosphere becomes heavy and unpleasant, you can use the practice of the cake to restore harmony in your family. First of all, breathe in and out three times to give yourself enough courage, and then look at your mother and say to her, "Mommy, Mommy." Your mother will ask you what you need to say and you will say, "I remember that we have a cake in the refrigerator." Whether or not there is really a cake in the refrigerator does not matter. The reason you say this is to help your parents have a way out of fighting.

Saying "there is a cake in the refrigerator" really means,

"Mama, Papa, don't make each other suffer any-more." When they hear these words, your parents will understand. Your mother will look at you and will say: "Quite right! My child, will you go out on the veranda and arrange the table and the chairs while I go and fetch the cake and the tea?" When mother says this, you have already found a way out of the danger-ous situation. You can run out on to the veranda and wait for her. Your mother now has an opportunity to withdraw from the fight with your father. Before you spoke up, she could not stand up and leave since it would be very impolite and it might pour more oil onto the flames of your father's anger. Now, she can go into the kitchen. As she opens the refrigerator to take out the cake and boils the water to make the tea, she can follow her breathing as she learned in Plum Village. If there is no real cake in the refrigerator, don't worry. Your mother is talented and she will find something to substitute for the cake. As she prepares the cake and tea, she can smile the half smile to feel lighter in body and spirit.

While father is sitting alone in the living room, he will recognize that his wife and child are practic-ing what they learned in Plum Village. He will think to himself: "If I don't practice, then it will look very strange. It will look as if I don't remember what we all learned together." He will also begin to practice breathing in mindfulness. Gradually, his hot temper will calm down, and he will begin to feel affection for his wife and child. After the tea and the cake have been placed on the table, he may walk out slowly onto the veranda to join the tea party with his wife and child in an atmosphere that is light and full of understanding. If Father is hesitant to come out, then you can run into the house, take Father's hand, hold it to your cheek, and coax him by saying, "Daddy, do you love me? Daddy, come and have some tea and cake with me."

If you do this, you will be bringing Plum Village back to your home, and life in the family will become peaceful.

Inviting the Bell

In the old days when there were no telephones, people who lived far apart were not able to talk to each other. When the telephone was invented, it was like a miracle. Now we are used to the telephone, so we don't see how wonderful it is. But it's really a miraculous invention. Every time we use the telephone and hear the voice of a loved one who lives far away, it can make us very happy.

The bell is a kind of telephone because listening to the sound of the bell is like listening to the voice of someone very dear. The sound of the bell is the voice of the Buddha, calling us home, reminding us to be more at peace with ourselves and with the world. We listen attentively to that voice. Listening to the bell can be very wonderful, and it can bring us a lot of peace and joy. It can bring us back to our true home.

When we are away from our true home for a long time, we long to return to it. In our true home, we feel at peace. We feel we don't have to run anywhere and that we are free of problems. We can relax and be ourselves. It's wonderful to be the way you are. You are already what you want to become. You don't need to be someone or something else.

Look at the apple tree. It's wonderful for the apple tree just to be the apple tree. It doesn't have to become something else. It's wonderful that I am myself, that you are yourself. We only need to let ourselves be what we already are, and enjoy ourselves just as we are. That feeling, that realization, is our true home. Each of us has a true home inside.

Our true home always calls to us, day and night, in a very clear voice. It keeps sending us waves of love and concern, but they don't reach us because we are so busy. So when we hear the sound of the bell, we remember that the bell is there to help us to go back to our true home, and we let go of everything—talking, thinking, playing, singing, being with friends, or even meditating! We give it all up and go back to our true home.

When we listen to the sound of the bell, the reason we don't talk or think or do anything is because we are listening to the voice of a person we love and respect a lot. Just stand quietly and listen with all your heart. If there are three sounds, listen and breathe deeply during the entire period. As you concentrate, you can say to yourself, "Breathing in, I feel fine; breathing out, I feel happy." Feeling happy is very important. What is the use of breathing and practicing if you don't feel well, if you don't feel happy? The deepest desire in each of us is to be happy and to bring happiness to the people and other beings around us.

You might like to invite the bell yourself. Here is how to do it. First, pick up the bell, leaving the bell cushion on the floor and using the palm of your hand as the cushion. Your open hand holding the bell looks very beautiful, like a chrysanthemum or a lotus flower with five petals. Our hand is the lotus and the bell is the precious jewel in the lotus. We can look at it and say, "Oh, the jewel in the lotus," or in Sanskrit, "*Om mani padme hum.*"

Hold the bell up in front of you, look at it, and smile. Then breathe in and out three times while you silently recite the following gatha:

Body, speech, and mind in perfect oneness,
I send my heart along with the sound of the bell.
May the hearers awaken from forgetfulness
And transcend the path of anxiety and sorrow.

It's okay if, as you ring the bell, you happen to forget the gatha, but do your best to remember it. As you breathe in, recite the first line:

Body, speech, and mind in perfect oneness.

This means you have concentration.

As you breathe out, recite the second line :

I send my heart along with the sound of this bell.

This means you send your love to the world.

With your next in-breath, recite:

May the hearers awaken from forgetfulness.

Forgetfulness is the opposite of mindfulness, and the sound
of the bell helps us to be mindful. Hearing the voice of the
Buddha, we come back to the present moment.

With your next out-breath, recite:

And transcend the path of anxiety and sorrow.

After you have practiced breathing in and out like this
while reciting the gatha, you will feel much better; your
mind and body are now united, you are concentrated, and
you have the beautiful wish that everyone who hears this
bell feels no sorrow, anger, or anxiety, and that they enjoy
breathing and smiling.

Now you are ready to invite the bell to sound. When inviting the bell, we always give a wake-up sound first to prepare
the bell and to prepare everyone for the full sound of the
bell that will follow, so that they are not surprised by it. We
make this by touching the bell inviter to the bell and leaving

it there as we breathe in; this is called "waking up the bell" or making a "half-sound" of the bell. Everyone stops thinking and talking and gets ready to receive the full sound of the bell.

Between the waking-up sound of the bell and its real sound is the space of one breath. So you practice breathing in while waiting for the real sound, and then invite the bell so that the real sound comes. We say "Invite the bell to sound," not "Hit" or "Strike the bell," because we want to be kind and not do violence to the bell.

Those who are listening to the sound of the bell silently recite the following gatha:

> Listen, listen,
> This wonderful sound brings me back to my true
>   home.

"Listen, listen" means we listen with all our concentration while we breathe in. While we breathe out, we smile and say, "This wonderful sound brings me back to my true home." And we listen to the sound of the bell, the voice of the Buddha inside, calling each of us back to our true home, the place of peace, tolerance, and love.

I Have Arrived

Thich Nhat Hanh
Arrangement by Betsy Rose

Moderately

I have ar - rived. I am home in the here, and in the now. I have ar- rived. I am home in the here, and in the now. I am sol - id, I am free. I am sol - id, I am free. In the ul - ti - mate I dwell. In the ul - ti - mate I dwell.

About Thich Nhat Hanh

Thich Nhat Hanh is a Zen Buddhist monk, a peacemaker, a poet, a storywriter, and a beloved teacher. Born in Vietnam, he became a novice monk at the age of sixteen. He is affectionately called Thay (teacher) by his friends and students.

Thay came to the United States during the Vietnam War in an effort to put an end to the fighting and bring peace to all countries involved. He now lives in Plum Village, a community of monks, nuns, and laypeople in southwest France. Each year, Thay travels to Europe, Asia, and North America to give retreats and lectures on the practice of mindfulness.

Old stone buildings, gardens, orchards, fields of sunflowers, and wonderful lotus ponds welcome visitors to Plum Village. People from all over the world come to practice mindful walking, eating, sitting, and breathing meditation. During summer retreats, Thay devotes the first part of his talks to young people. He also invites children to participate in the many enjoyable, mindful activities offered at Plum Village, including pebble meditation, music, art, drama, and games.

Plum Blossom Books publishes books for young people on mindfulness and Buddhism by Thich Nhat Hanh and other authors. For a complete list of titles for children, or a free copy of our catalog, please write us or visit our website:

Plum Blossom Books • Parallax Press
P.O. Box 7355, Berkeley, CA 94707
Tel: (510) 525-0101
www.parallax.org

Monastics and laypeople practice the art of mindful living in the tradition of Thich Nhat Hanh at retreat communities in France and the United States. To reach any of these communities, or for information about individuals and families joining for a practice period, please contact:

Plum Village
13 Martineau
33580 Dieulivol, France
www.plumvillage.org

Blue Cliff Monastery
3 Mindfulness Road
Pine Bush, NY 12566
www.bluecliffmonastery.org

Deer Park Monastery
2499 Melru Lane
Escondido, CA 92026
www.deerparkmonastery.org

The Mindfulness Bell, a journal of the art of mindful living in the tradition of Thich Nhat Hanh, is published three times a year by Plum Village. To subscribe or to see the worldwide directory of Sanghas, visit www.mindfulnessbell.org

Other Children's Books from Parallax Press and Plum Blossom Books

Anh's Anger

The Coconut Monk

The Dragon Prince

Each Breath a Smile

The Hermit and the Well

Meow Said the Mouse